**Effec**
for E

Introduction

How would you feel if I told you that the way you revise is probably ineffective? And that the techniques you're using mean you might struggle to remember the important things you need to know for your exams? You'd be worried, right? And, no doubt, you'd want me to tell you where you were going wrong, as well as pointing out what revision strategies actually work?

Well, you're in luck. In this guide, I'm going to let you in on the secrets of psychology and cognitive science (the study of how humans think and learn). I'm going to show you where most students are going wrong. Then I'm going to introduce you to the study skills that are most likely to help you do brilliantly in your exams.

Once we've grasped the basics of effective revision, we'll investigate how you can apply these techniques to your English revision.

Along the way, we'll look at each stage of the revision process to ensure you perform really well in this vital subject. I'll show you how I teach my students to master their English revision, as well as giving you examples of what really successful students do to help them towards top grades in GCSE English.

Can you really revise for English?

My students regularly tell me that they find it hard to know how to revise for English. They find revising for Maths and Science much easier. They'll sometimes even say *You can't really revise for English, can you?* This guide will show you why that common belief is wrong. It will show you that all you need is an organised, step-by-step approach to your English revision. So, if you feel like you don't know how to revise, especially for English, you've come to the right place.

Where most students go wrong with revision

How do you begin revising for English? Let me guess. You get out your class notes – from your exercise book, or poetry anthology – and you re-read them. As well as this, you go back and read revision guides again. As you read your notes, you highlight the really important information you wrote down in class or the key parts of your revision guide.

Am I right?

If you do this, you're not alone. But, I'm sorry to say, if you are revising in this way, you might well be limiting your chances of adding facts and ideas to your long-term memory.

Back in 2013, an important piece of research[1] summarised the effectiveness of the most popular revision strategies used by students. The researchers found a big problem with two techniques that students love to use: re-reading and highlighting of notes. These strategies, they found, wasted valuable revision time and didn't really help students remember things in the long run.

So, what's the problem with these two favourite revision methods?

Re-reading your notes doesn't really work

✗ Re-reading your notes doesn't help your understanding of what you read.

✗ Any benefits you get are probably not long-term.

✗ You might remember things soon after re-reading, but you might forget, or not really understand, what you've just read over.

Highlighting isn't as helpful as you think

✗ Students usually mark too much text when highlighting.

✗ This means it doesn't stand out so is less likely to be remembered.

✗ Picking out the main points of a topic is trickier than you think.

Collins

You can't revise
for GCSE English!

YES

YOU

CAN

and Mark Roberts
shows you how

Contents

Please let me keep my highlighter!

If your little neon friends make you feel comfortable while reading, then I'm not going to suggest that you stick your highlighters in the bin! But if you're going to use them, make sure you recognise that highlighting can only be the first step of your revision journey. After highlighting, you'll need to move on to techniques that have more benefit.

Does your highlighting look like this?

So what really works when revising?

According to the evidence from cognitive science, the two most effective revision strategies are **retrieval practice** and **spaced practice**.

Retrieval practice involves a test to see what you can remember about a particular subject. Crucially, to do this properly, this test has to be done without notes or other revision materials.

Forcing ourselves us to recall information from memory is a really effective revision technique. When you start doing retrieval activities, though, you might not enjoy them!

To begin with, retrieval practice feels much more challenging than reading over your notes, or highlighting sections of a revision guide. But over time, as you test yourself you'll start to feel more confident.

The first thing you'll notice is that retrieval practice allows you to see the gaps in your knowledge. For example, you might think that you understood a particular poem really well when you covered it in class, but when you quiz yourself without your anthology notes, you discover that you can't remember any quotations.

Secondly, the struggle of remembering information actually strengthens your long-term memory.

Things are far more likely to be remembered if you've had to pluck them from your mind rather than having the answer before your eyes. The effort of putting yourself on the spot really is worth the uncomfortable feeling of not being able to answer questions you thought you could. What's more, researchers have also found that retrieval practice works well in preparing you to remember key information even in really stressful tests.

So, using this technique should help you to recall what you've learnt in the high pressure situation of an exam hall.

Retrieval practice – testing for a better memory

✔ Practice tests can give a big boost to your learning.

✔ All you need is a pen and some index cards.

✔ It works just as well self-quizzing or paired up with a friend.

✔ You can even create index cards in class as you take notes.

✔ Feels difficult but helps you prepare for the pressure of a GCSE exam.

What does a good GCSE English flashcard look like?

When creating revision flashcards, remember the following tips:
- Include a question on one side and answers or definitions on the other side.
- Double check the answer(s) – you don't want to remember something that's incorrect by mistake.

Take a look at this excellent example:

> *Why is the motif of blood significant*
> *in Macbeth?*

> 1. Presence of blood acts as an obvious reminder
>   of injury and death.
> 2. Reminds characters of the consequences of
>   their actions.
> 3. Imaginary blood is even more important—
>   blood becomes symbolic of guilt.
> 4. Eventually, bloody hands motif is linked to
>   escalating madness.

How should I use flashcards during retrieval practice?

The most important things to remember when using flashcards are:

- You must include a decent pause before checking the answer. Resist the temptation to flip it over quickly. If you fail to leave a pause while you're thinking, you'll miss out on the long-term memory boost that comes with this technique.
- Pay particular attention to the cards that you struggle with the most. Put these at the back of your pile to ensure that you have another go at recalling the answer. If you still have no idea after two or three attempts, you'll have to go back and check your more detailed class notes, or ask your teacher to go over this with you again.
- Don't forget to go back over the cards you found easy first time. The research suggests that, even with ones you could answer quickly to begin with, there is a clear benefit of testing yourself with them again and again.

Spaced practice is when a student spreads out their revision in shorter sessions over a longer period of time, rather than trying to revise everything in marathon sessions.

For example, you might study one different character from *An Inspector Calls* over a few weeks before your mock exam, rather than trying to study all of the play's characters the night before.

Students do tend to revise by going over all the information in one long revision session, commonly known as cramming. But the research shows that this is a really bad way to study because the material doesn't move from your working memory to your long-term memory. What's more, cramming is stressful and tends to eat into your precious sleep.

With spaced practice, the opposite occurs: because you are frequently revisiting your learning in small chunks, it is far more likely to stick in the long run and you are far more likely to feel less anxious before an exam.

You'll still need to study the night before an important test, but you won't need to spend hours frantically trying to re-learn something you haven't covered for ages.

Spaced practice versus cramming

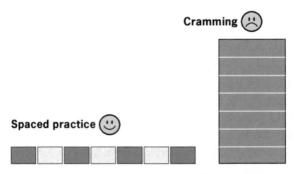

An important part of spaced practice is making sure that as well as going back over things that you have studied in the last lesson, you also make sure you revisit things that you covered three days, a week, and a month ago.

Combine this with retrieval practice and you will be using a potent mix of the most effective study techniques.

Start with the older material first. For example, you might have put some flashcards to one side a couple of weeks ago, feeling confident that you had remembered everything on them. Go through them again and see if you can still recall things as fluently as before.

For maximum benefit, revise the material you learn in class throughout the year, not just when you have an assessment on the horizon. Little and often, varying the gaps between when you go back over a topic, is the way to go for the best results.

Spaced practice – gaps between learning to make things stick

✓ Regularly revisiting your learning helps you remember things in the long-term.

✓ Put aside a bit of time for your English revision each day, not just near a test.

✓ Vary the things that you revise and don't forget stuff you haven't done for a while.

✓ Works much better than cramming and is far less stressful!

❝ Top 5 to thrive

1. Most students use ineffective revision strategies.
2. Re-reading and highlighting aren't good ways to revise.
3. Retrieval practice feels difficult to begin with but really helps you remember key information.
4. Flashcards are brilliant for revising English, but use them carefully.
5. Space out your revision schedule for maximum impact.

❞

Organising your notes and annotations

Students who take notes in class while listening to the teacher typically do better in exams than those who don't. Taking notes gives you a better chance of remembering the content of the lesson. What's more, creating your own notes has a more positive impact on your long-term learning than being given a set of notes by the teacher.

But there's a problem with note-taking.

It seems straightforward but it's actually quite tricky to master.

Listening, picking out the most important information, and writing it down at the same time, can be pretty difficult. And these notes are going to be the basis of your all-important revision schedule.

So it's vital that you learn how to make notes that will be helpful when you come to use them for your revision.

Note-taking in class – common mistakes to avoid

Here are some of the things that can go wrong when you take notes in class:

- Trying to copy down everything on the board.
- Trying to copy down everything the teacher says.
- The teacher talks much quicker than you can write.

When you attempt to copy down all possible information, it stops you listening carefully.

This prevents you getting a good understanding of the main points of the topic. It's easy to see why students fall into these traps: nobody ever shows them how to take notes effectively!

It needn't be like this.

I'm going to introduce you to a note-taking method that will allow you to organise your notes. That will enable you to record the most important ideas and vocabulary. That will give you a better chance of creating notes good enough to use as a basis for your revision. Then, later on in this section, I'm going to show you how a really successful student has taken this note-taking approach to a different level.

Cornell notes – the answer to your note-taking problems

The Cornell notes method was created by Walter Pauk, a professor of education at Cornell University, in the 1940s. Once you get the hang of it, it's easy to use. It may seem simple but it can have a big impact on the quality of your notes and your overall achievement.

Let's have a look at what you need to do when taking notes.

Firstly, get the right layout on your page:

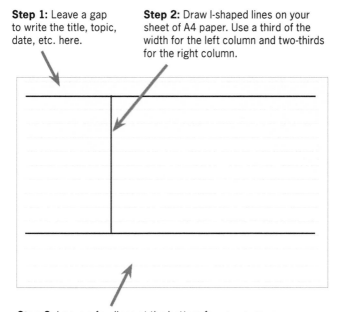

Step 1: Leave a gap to write the title, topic, date, etc. here.

Step 2: Draw l-shaped lines on your sheet of A4 paper. Use a third of the width for the left column and two-thirds for the right column.

Step 3: Leave a few lines at the bottom for your summary.

Next, follow the method of what to write and where to write it:

Step 4: Write your notes during the lesson.

Step 5: Think of a question that your notes will help you to answer. Use a statement if you can't think of a question.

Step 6: Write a short summary of what you've covered on the page.

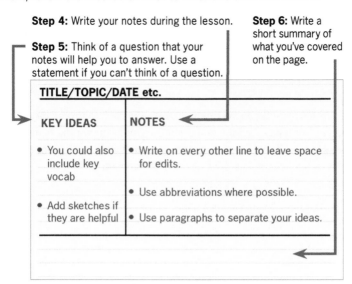

TITLE/TOPIC/DATE etc.

KEY IDEAS	NOTES
• You could also include key vocab • Add sketches if they are helpful	• Write on every other line to leave space for edits. • Use abbreviations where possible. • Use paragraphs to separate your ideas.

Here's an example of what a page, using the Cornell notes format, might look like:

Wilfred Owen – early life and war experiences – 11/2/2020	
Did Owen have a religious upbringing?	Wilfred was brought up by parents who were both devout Christians.
Owen wanted to be a priest	1911 – went to live at Dunsden Vicarage, with a view to becoming a priest. But suffered a loss of faith and left.
What effect did WW1 have on his faith?	The horrors of WW1 further eradicated Owen's belief in God. Links to the line 'for love of God seems dying' in 'Exposure' being ambiguous. The men might have lost God's love but their love for him is also dying.

- Owen was given a conventional Christian upbringing.
- Wanted to train as a priest but lost his faith.
- WW1's carnage further damaged his belief. Links to key quotation in 'Exposure'.

The importance of vocabulary

Writing down key vocabulary when taking notes is really important. It should become an important part of your analysis of literature texts.

A key idea in 'Exposure', for example, is the painful wait for action ('But nothing happens') that might ironically lead to death. An excellent word for when there is a lack of movement or action is the noun 'inertia'.

Adding this to your vocabulary list on your Cornell notes sheet should eventually allow you to write sentences like:

> *For Owen, the true enemy is not the opposing army, or even the biting wind. Instead, it is the inertia, and the fear that accompanies it, that torments the soldiers.*

Even better, these words can be used in your own creative writing. Writing about 'the inertia of the government' sounds much better than 'the government haven't done anything'.

How to get the most out of your Cornell notes

I asked my ex-student, Molly Bolding, how she uses Cornell notes. Molly did brilliantly in her GCSE English and is now studying English at Cambridge University.

Her top tips are:
- Write your ideas out clearly, in full sentences, in the notes section.
- Paragraph properly to separate your ideas out.
- Include plenty of detail – you'll be coming back to this in revision, so the more you write now the more helpful this will be.
- In class, you only need to fill in the notes section. Wait until your revision time to complete the question and summary sections.
- If you can't think of a question, use a short statement – either way, it should prompt you to think of the notes you have written in full.
- Don't include too much information in the question/statement.
- Write your summary section in a different colour. When you're skimming through your book looking for a certain topic, it'll be easier to find the relevant summary.

Using Cornell notes for retrieval practice

Having notes that are clear, concise and organised really helps with retrieval practice. Let's see how the earlier notes page example – focusing on the war poet Wilfred Owen's attitude to religion – can be easily turned into a flashcard:

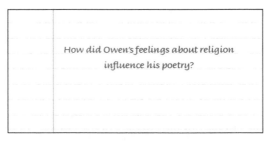

How did Owen's feelings about religion
influence his poetry?

- Owen was given a conventional Christian upbringing.
- Wanted to train to be a priest at Dunstan in 1911, but lost his faith.
- The carnage he witnessed in WW1 further damaged his belief.
- Links to the line 'for love of God seems dying' in 'Exposure' being ambiguous. The men might have lost God's love but their love for him is also dying.

But, as Molly points out, if your Cornell notes are really good, you can use them for retrieval practice without always having to turn them into flashcards. Here's how she does it:

Using Cornell notes for quick retrieval practice

✓ Open your book to the relevant page of ideas and read through it.

✓ Cover the notes section with another sheet of paper so that you can only see the questions column.

✓ Practise reading the questions, and either saying or writing out the notes that answer that question.

✓ Don't worry about memorising exactly what you wrote in the notes section, just hold onto the key information or ideas.

- ✓ Asking yourself what you wrote about pushes your brain to make connections between the key words of the question and those in your notes.

- ✓ Feels difficult but makes it much easier to recall the information in the future.

Taking your Cornell notes to the next level

Ok, so you've tried out the Cornell notes process. You've now got the hang of organising your notes in this really helpful way. It's also helped with your ongoing revision through retrieval practice.

But Cornell notes aren't just helpful for taking notes while listening to your English teacher in class. Molly also uses them when she is reading other resources – like lesson handouts, revision guides or what critics have said about the literature texts – to organise her notes. She finds these notes just as helpful as the ones she writes in class. Take a look at an example of how you can use this approach too. Imagine your teacher has given you the following handout to annotate (during a lesson or to read for homework):

Jekyll and Hyde – influence of Darwinism

On the surface, Dr Jekyll is a good character, respectable and gentlemanly. By sharp contrast, Mr Hyde is pure evil, a monstrous murderer who kills purely because he feels like it. Beneath the surface, however, this antithesis is not that straightforward. Rather than being a story purely about good versus evil, *Jekyll and Hyde* can also be seen in terms of the difference between evolution and degeneration.

In 1871, Charles Darwin published *The Descent of Man*, coming to the conclusion that men had 'descended from a hairy, tailed quadruped'. Darwin's theory of evolution horrified sections of Victorian society by challenging not just religious beliefs about our creation but also the elevated view of humankind's biological superiority.

Stevenson's portrayal of Hyde as a grotesque and disgusting being taps into these fears. Mr Hyde is seen by those that he encounters as 'downright detestable' but might this be a result of him reminding those that he meets, in a subconscious way, of their own primitive evolutionary background?

Using Cornell notes to annotate your reading, like Molly, could help you come up with something like this:

Jekyll and Hyde – Darwinism and Mr Hyde – 17/3/2020	
How does Darwin's theory influence our reading of the novel?	By using Darwin's theory of evolution, we can see beyond a simplistic 'good versus evil' reading of the novel. On a deeper level, we can view Jekyll and Hyde as being about the contrast between evolution and degeneration.
Why do characters find Hyde so 'detestable'?	In Hyde, they possibly see something that subconsciously reminds them of their primitive evolution? The uncivilised part that lurks within us all.

- Jekyll = good, and Hyde = evil is too simplistic.
- Darwinism helps us see it as evolution vs degeneration.
- Hyde reminds them of the primitive side we all have.

I prefer to write over the actual handout – how should I annotate?

The key thing to remember, as we saw in the first chapter, is that underlining and highlighting alone is not enough. To end up with decent annotations you can revise from, make sure that you:

- Pick out key bits of information and explain why they're important.
- Summarise and explain ideas and concepts in your own words.
- Write questions and statements, using the underlined/highlighted parts to answer these.
- Write down definitions of key vocabulary, including helpful synonyms.
- Make links to relevant parts of the text.

Here's what this might look like:

IMPORTANT FOR THEME OF DUALITY! Good vs evil reading of the novel is simplistic. Darwin's theory allows us to see Jekyll and Hyde in terms of evolution vs degeneration.

Jekyll and Hyde – influence of Darwinism

On the surface, Dr Jekyll is a good character, respectable and gentlemanly. By sharp contrast, Mr Hyde is pure evil, a monstrous murderer who kills purely because he feels like it. Beneath the surface, however, this antithesis is not that straightforward. <u>Rather than being a story purely about good versus evil, *Jekyll and Hyde* can also be seen in terms of the difference between evolution and degeneration.</u>

In 1871, Charles Darwin published *The Descent of Man*, coming to the conclusion that men had 'descended from a hairy, tailed quadruped'. Darwin's theory of evolution horrified sections of Victorian society by challenging not just religious beliefs about our creation but also the elevated view of humankind's biological superiority.

Stevenson's portrayal of <u>Hyde as a grotesque and disgusting</u> being taps into these fears. Mr Hyde is seen by those that he encounters as 'downright detestable' but <u>might this be a result of him reminding those that he meets, in a subconscious way, of their own primitive evolutionary background?</u>

Link to Enfield's description pg.10

Why do other characters find Hyde so 'detestable'?

Starting your revision of a topic with highly effective notes like these will greatly increase your confidence. Contrast the notes above with what you end up with when you just underline while annotating:

Jekyll and Hyde – influence of Darwinism

On the surface, Dr Jekyll is a good character, respectable and gentlemanly. By sharp contrast, Mr Hyde is pure evil, a monstrous murderer who kills purely because he feels like it. Beneath the surface, however, this antithesis is not that straightforward. <u>Rather than being a story purely about good versus evil, *Jekyll and Hyde* can also be seen in terms of the difference between evolution and degeneration.</u>

In 1871, Charles Darwin published *The Descent of Man*, coming to the conclusion that men had 'descended from a hairy, tailed quadruped'. Darwin's theory of evolution horrified sections of Victorian society by challenging not just religious beliefs about our creation but also the elevated view of humankind's biological superiority.

Stevenson's portrayal of <u>Hyde as a grotesque and disgusting</u> being taps into these fears. Mr Hyde is seen by those that he encounters as 'downright detestable' but <u>might this be a result of him reminding those that he meets, in a subconscious way, of their own primitive evolutionary background?</u>

Hopefully, you can see that these lines on the page will be next to useless during revision. You'll have little idea why you highlighted these parts of the text and what you were thinking at the time.

What about annotating poems?

My students find taking notes on poetry quite tricky. When we first study a poem, they tend to write down everything they learn about it, covering every inch of the page in a rainbow of highlighted colours. Or they write down just a couple of words and end up lacking detail.

For this reason, I think the 'brain dump' approach to poetry note-taking is really important.

Brain dump is a type of retrieval practice where you start with a blank page and simply write down everything you know about the topic you're revising. I find that using this technique with an unannotated poem is a really good way of finding out (a) what you've remembered, and (b) the parts of the poem that you understand the best. An example of brain dump annotation for 'Sonnet 43' by Elizabeth Barrett Browning might look like this:

Hypophora reveals immediate, detailed answer to central question

> How do I love thee? Let me count the ways.
> I love thee to the depth and breadth and height
> My soul can reach, when feeling out of sight
> For the ends of being and ideal grace.
> I love thee to the level of every day's
> Most quiet need, by sun and candle-light.
> I love thee freely, as men strive for right.
> I love thee purely, as they turn from praise.
> I love thee with the passion put to use
> In my old griefs, and with my childhood's faith.
> I love thee with a love I seemed to lose
> With my lost saints. I love thee with the breath,
> Smiles, tears, of all my life; and, if God choose,
> I shall but love thee better after death.

Her love, like Juliet's for Romeo, is boundless and infinite

Hints at a dilution of her Christian faith – implies this love may offer greater fulfilment

Key idea – romantic love has the capacity to move us to a transcendental and spiritual place

Contrast alludes to 'in sickness and in health' commitment of marriage

The students can now improve and develop these annotations by going back over their original annotations. They can then brain dump again until they narrow down their notes to the key ideas they will need to remember for the exams.

66 Top 5 to thrive

1. Most students find note-taking during lessons a real struggle.

2. Cornell notes help you make excellent notes for retrieval practice.

3. The quality of the notes you take in class will have a big impact on your understanding of topics in revision.

4. You can also improve your annotations while reading handouts and textbooks by using Cornell notes.

5. Just highlighting and underlining is not enough – annotate with summaries, questions and statements.

Memorising quotes

My students often feel anxious about memorising quotes for the English literature exams. They recognise that being able to recall quotes from the text is really important. They know that without this knowledge base they won't be able to answer exam questions effectively. They worry that when it matters most, sat in the exam without their copy of the text as a comfort blanket, they'll forget most of the important lines.

This is an understandable concern. After all, depending on what exam board you are doing, you'll need to remember important quotes to help answer questions on the novels, plays and poems that you study.

How many quotes do I need to memorise?

For novels and plays, you're going to need several key quotes for each of the key characters and each of the main themes. You'll also need a few quotes that can help you answer possible questions on setting and dramatic techniques.

For the poetry anthology, you'll probably need to know three or four key quotes for all the poems from the poetry anthology. That's for each of the 15 poems from AQA, OCR and Edexcel. Or 18 poems for Eduqas. That's a lot of quotes to remember!

How can I possibly manage all that?

You're going to need to be organised. You'll need to do a little bit of English revision on most days. A revision schedule that involves cramming simply won't work. Learning all these quotes at the last minute, as the exam approaches, just isn't going to happen. When it comes to memorising enough quotes to be able to do well in English exams, short and regular sessions of retrieval practice – from the start of your GCSE course – is the only way forward. The numbers of quotes you'll need to know might seem daunting to begin with. But with frequent short bursts of practice, you'll be surprised at how much you can recall. Then you'll start feeling much more confident.

Getting started

STEP 1: Choosing the right quotes

To begin with, decide which quotes you're going to learn. In Chapter 5, we'll take a look at 'killer quotes' – quotes from texts that are so important, and so versatile, that they can be used in virtually any essay. But, for now, the best thing you can do is choose your own list of quotes, rather than taking somebody else's list from a website. If you have a sheet from your teacher, don't feel that you can only use these recommended quotes. The reason for this is that you will be the one writing about the quotes. You'll need to understand them. And you'll need to feel confident that you have plenty of interesting and thoughtful things to say about them.

Start with a longer list of possible quotes, then think what you could write about each:

- Does it contain interesting key words to focus on?
- Can you explain the impact of any language features?
- Is this quote structurally significant?
- Will this quote allow you the opportunity to discuss relevant context?
- What does this particular quote reveal about a character?
- How exactly might it illustrate a key theme?
- (Where relevant) does this quote provide me with an opportunity to compare with quotes from other texts?

Let's take a look at an example list for the character Gerald Croft from *An Inspector Calls* (the ones highlighted have been selected by the student as the most useful quotes):

Gerald Croft key quotes
- 'You couldn't have done anything else.'
- 'We're respectable citizens and not criminals.'
- 'I've told you – I was awfully busy at the works all that time.'
- 'I drink to you – and hope I can make you as happy as you deserve to be.'
- 'unless Eric's been up to something. And that would be very awkward wouldn't it?'
- 'All right, I knew her. Let's leave it at that.'
- 'It was all over and done with, last summer. I hadn't set eyes on the girl for at least six months. I don't come into this suicide business.'
- 'It's bound to be unpleasant and disturbing.'
- 'You've been through it, and now you want to see someone else put through it.'

- 'The palace music hall... is a favourite haunt of women of the town.'
- 'Sorry – I – well, I've suddenly realised – taken it in properly – that she's dead.'
- 'I insisted on Daisy moving into those rooms and I made her take some money to keep her going there.'
- 'I became at once the most important person in her life.'
- 'So I broke it off definitely... she was – very gallant – about it.'
- 'But how do you know it's the same girl?... We've no proof it was the same photograph and therefore no proof it was the same girl.'
- 'Everything's all right now Sheila. What about this ring?'

STEP 2: Creating a bank of flashcards

Over time, you'll need to do the same for each main character and theme for each text. You'll also need to do the same for things like setting and dramatic techniques. Then a selection of quotes for each poem. As you do this, transfer your list of quotes on to flashcards like this:

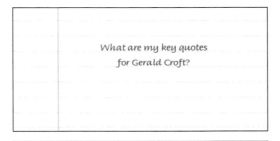

What are my key quotes
for Gerald Croft?

1. 'I've told you – I was awfully busy at the works all that time.'
2. 'It's bound to be unpleasant and disturbing.'
3. 'Sorry – I – well, I've suddenly realised – taken it in properly – that she's dead.'
4. 'I insisted on Daisy moving into those rooms and I made her take some money to keep her going there.'
5. 'Everything's all right now Sheila. What about this ring?'

In the next chapter, I'll show you how you can use flashcards to develop your knowledge of each key quote. But to start with, test yourself on them to ensure you can remember which quotes you're going to use for each character, theme, etc.

A great way to help remember key quotes is to use pictograms instead of words.

Pictograms are visual symbols that represent people, objects or words. Look at the following example pictograms. I'm sure you understand what each one means, despite the lack of words:

Research has shown that using pictograms instead of, or in addition to, words can improve your chances of being able to recall information in a memory test[1].

As with standard retrieval practice, the initial struggle of remembering increases the chances of making the quote stick. My students find pictograms really tough to begin with, but after a few goes they are surprised by how many they can recall. Here are a few that I created for key quotes from *Romeo and Juliet*:

If you're studying *Romeo and Juliet*, hopefully you managed to get one or two right. Even if you don't do that play, you might've found yourself having a go at identifying the odd word. That's the thing about pictograms: they can be frustrating and cryptic but they're also fun and addictive!

The answers are:

1. 'Parting is such sweet sorrow'
2. 'A plague o' [on] both your houses!'
3. 'O, she doth teach the torches to burn bright'

Have a go at creating your own pictograms. Like me, you can easily use icons, images and clip art that you find online, then stick them on your flashcards. Or you can simply draw your own, straight onto a card.

Either way, thinking about how to visually represent the words will help lodge them in your long-term memory – especially when you come back to them a few weeks later and have to strain to remember what your pictograms are meant to mean.

How else can I use images to help me remember the texts?

There is strong evidence to suggest that using dual coding really helps you to remember things you've learnt.

Dual coding is a technique that uses images and words together, giving you two ways of recalling the information you've learnt later on. As well as using pictograms, you can also use drawings to help you remember things like the plot.

This is an example for *Romeo and Juliet*:

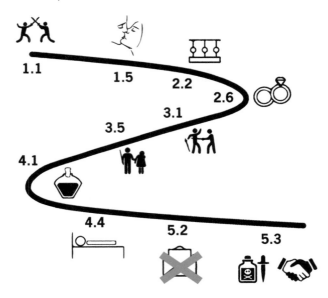

Using images from the text for analysis

Head of English Chris Curtis advises his students to memorise certain key images from the texts they study. These are easier to remember than full quotes, so really help with your analysis with relatively little effort.

For example:

- At the start of *An Inspector Calls*, Priestley uses the glass of port as a symbol of…
- Throughout the novella *Jekyll and Hyde*, locked doors are used to represent the theme of…
- In *Lord of the Flies*, the conch is used to symbolise…

STEP 4: Narrowing down to single words

Sometimes, when we're trying to learn quotes, we fall into the trap of trying to memorise really long chunks of text. In some cases, single words can do a really powerful job, as well as being easier to memorise. For this reason, Chris Curtis encourages his classes to remember lots of single-word quotes. He gives an example for Scrooge from *A Christmas Carol* that will enable you to 'track the development of character through the use of three words'[2]:

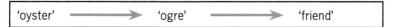

By choosing certain important words from the texts that you study, you can start to make better links across the text as a whole.

You might, for example, look at three negative single words (beginning with 'un') from *Macbeth* and consider how they add to your understanding of the development of Lady Macbeth's character:

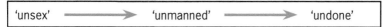

As well as helping you track character development, revising single-word quotes is an excellent way of adding an extra layer of challenge into your retrieval practice. Firstly, write down a list of ten single-word quotes. Then you have to use each key word as a prompt to remember the wider quote. To make it really useful, make sure you are using spaced practice by including texts that you haven't studied for a while, as well as ones you've looked at very recently. Also, for extra difficulty, use quotes from all the texts that you're studying.

For example, you might create a list of single-word quotes that all begin with the letter S:

1. sweet
2. signature
3. sunlight
4. Sellotape
5. squat
6. shipwreck
7. suddenly
8. sabre
9. sneer
10. sheath

Then, come back to this list in a few days, a week, a month, three months and so on, seeing if you can recall the full quote.

In case you're wondering, the quotes in this list are taken from *Romeo and Juliet*, *Jekyll and Hyde* and AQA's *Power and Conflict* poetry anthology:

1. sweet ('O sweet Juliet, Thy beauty hath made me effeminate.') *Romeo and Juliet*
2. signature ('if ever I read Satan's signature upon a face') *Jekyll and Hyde*
3. sunlight ('I am branded by an impression of sunlight') 'The Émigrée'
4. Sellotape ('Sellotape bandaged around my hand') 'Poppies'
5. squat ('we build our houses squat') 'Storm on the Island'
6. shipwreck ('doomed to such a dreadful shipwreck') *Jekyll and Hyde*
7. suddenly ('suddenly he awoke and was running') 'Bayonet Charge'
8. sabre ('Flashe'd all their sabres bare') 'Charge of the Light Brigade'
9. sneer ('sneer of cold command') 'Ozymandias'
10. sheath ('This is thy sheath. There rust and let me die.') *Romeo and Juliet*

STEP 5: Developing your revision of single-word quotes

As you make your lists, you'll start to notice that certain words crop up more than once in the same text. For example, in *Romeo and Juliet*, the adjective 'sweet' is used to refer to Juliet on 16 occasions. In *Merchant of Venice*, the word 'ducats' (gold coins) is also used regularly. In *Macbeth*, 'blood' is used more than 40 times. Look at the texts you study and consider the following:

- Which frequently used words act as a motif throughout the novel/ play/poem?
- What patterns do you notice about the quotes that use these words?
- How can these 'trigger words' help you to remember more quotes?

- How might these words help you gain a better understanding of the entire text?

In addition to cropping up repeatedly in the same text, certain key words will also appear in more than one text that you study. Take a look at the following list for example:

1. blind
2. grave
3. black
4. ache
5. fear
6. doomed
7. someone
8. hand(s)
9. peace
10. plague

Now, notice how some of these words feature lots of times across the texts *Romeo and Juliet*, *Jekyll and Hyde*, the modern play *DNA* and AQA's *Power and Conflict* poetry anthology:

1. blind ('blind me to me own identity' – 'Checking Out Me History'; 'If love be blind, love cannot hit the mark' – *Romeo and Juliet*)
2. grave ('My grave is like to be my wedding bed', 'Ask for me tomorrow and you shall find me a grave man', 'I would the fool were married to her grave!' – all *Romeo and Juliet*; 'wear a more than commonly grave countenance before the public' – *Jekyll and Hyde*)
3. black ('A huge peak, black and huge' – 'The Prelude'; 'This day's black fate on more days doth depend' – *Romeo and Juliet*; 'his face became suddenly black and the features seemed to melt and alter' – *Jekyll and Hyde*)
4. ache ('Our brains ache, in the merciless iced east winds that knife us' – 'Exposure')
5. fear ('it is a huge nothing we fear' – 'Storm on the Island'; 'In every Infants cry of fear' – 'London'; 'Phil. I'm scared, they scare me, this place, everyone, the fear' – *DNA*)
6. doomed ('doomed to such a dreadful shipwreck' – *Jekyll and Hyde*; 'D'you think we're doomed to behave like people before us did?' – *DNA*)
7. someone ('someone had blundered' – 'Charge of the Light Brigade'; 'to do what someone must' – 'War Photographer'; 'And someone's pegged a stone at him' – *DNA*)

8. **hands** ('his bloody life in my bloody hands' – 'Remains'; 'his hands, which did not tremble then/though seem to now' – 'War Photographer'; 'Was he the hand pointing that second?' – 'Bayonet Charge'; 'Sellotape bandaged around my hand' – 'Poppies'; 'where a hand/has written in the names and histories' – 'Tissue'; 'The hand that mocked them' – 'Ozymandias'; 'the hand that lay on my knee was corded and hairy' – *Jekyll and Hyde*; 'O, then, dear saint, let lips do what hands do', 'Where civil blood makes civil hands unclean' – *Romeo and Juliet*)

9. **peace** ('drawn, and talk of peace? I hate the word' – *Romeo and Juliet*)

10. **plague** ('a plague o' both your houses' – *Romeo and Juliet*; 'And blights with plagues the Marriage hearse' – 'London')

Hopefully, you can see how useful these lists can be for your revision of quotes. You can even group single-word quotes on a particular theme, like these based on AQA's *Love and Relationships* poetry anthology:

1. smile
2. lips
3. kiss
4. mouth
5. speak

With these kinds of strategies, memorising quotes shouldn't be too difficult or too stressful. Once you start to remember parts of important quotes, you'll realise that, with practice, the rest usually follows. And even if it doesn't, one interesting word on its own can often be enough.

66 Top 5 to thrive

1. You'll need to know lots of quotes for English exams, so don't leave it too late.

2. Choose quotes that you understand well and have plenty to write about.

3. Use flashcards and retrieval practice to memorise your lists of quotes.

4. Pictograms and drawings with words are a great way of remembering key quotes and scenes.

5. Single-word quotes are really helpful – use them as a springboard for recalling more than one quote at a time.

99

Exploding your quotes

By now, you should be starting to get better at remembering quotes for the exam. Hopefully, you can recall key quotes from the text more fluently. You'll still have a few tricky characters and themes for which you're struggling to find good quotes. But, on the whole, you've probably managed to memorise far more quotes than you thought possible. Well done!

Just knowing lots of quotes, however, isn't enough. Being able to recall quotes is really important. But knowing quotes is only a stepping stone towards brilliant written analysis. If you're going to fly in your exams, you'll need to have detailed plans of what you're going to say about the quotes that you've learnt.

What does 'exploding quotes' mean?

An explosion involves an object being blown into smaller pieces. As the object explodes, more and more pieces of it become visible.

So, when English teachers talk about **exploding quotes** they are talking metaphorically. In this case, the phrase is a really helpful way of thinking about key quotes. When you explode quotes, you're thinking about all the important things you can write about. Like an explosion, your annotations will get bigger as you focus in on small, but significant, parts of the quote.

Exploding quotes – exploring ideas for deeper analysis

✓ Allows you to plan your analysis ahead of the exam.

✓ Makes sure you don't just know the quote – you know what you're going to write about it.

✓ Helps you work out which quotes you are best at analysing.

✓ Encourages you to fully develop your analysis, helping you get higher marks.

How do I get started?

Grab a pile of flashcards, which you've used to memorise quotes for a particular text. For example, you might pick up a card on the character Snowball from the novel *Animal Farm*:

What are my key quotes
for Snowball?

1. 'it was Snowball who was best at writing.'
2. 'Without halting for a second, Snowball flung fifteen stone against Jones's legs.'
3. 'Until now the animals had been about equally divided in their sympathies, but in a moment Snowball's eloquence had carried them away.'
4. 'when the key of the store-shed was lost, the whole farm was convinced that Snowball had thrown it down the well... they went on believing this even after the mislaid key was found.'

Then choose a key quote and start to explode it on a piece of A4 paper, like this:

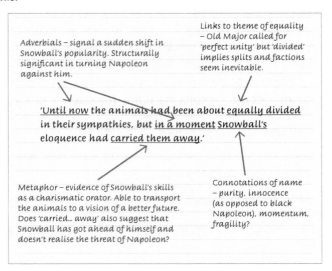

Adverbials – signal a sudden shift in Snowball's popularity. Structurally significant in turning Napoleon against him.

Links to theme of equality – Old Major called for 'perfect unity' but 'divided' implies splits and factions seem inevitable.

'Until now the animals had been about equally divided in their sympathies, but in a moment Snowball's eloquence had carried them away.'

Metaphor – evidence of Snowball's skills as a charismatic orator. Able to transport the animals to a vision of a better future. Does 'carried... away' also suggest that Snowball has got ahead of himself and doesn't realise the threat of Napoleon?

Connotations of name – purity, innocence (as opposed to black Napoleon), momentum, fragility?

What kind of things should I pick out?

When exploding your quotes, you should aim to make developed notes about the sort of things you'll be expected to write about in your analytical paragraphs.

This might include:

- Language features (metaphor, simile, rhetorical questions, hyperbole, repetition, etc.)
- Key word(s)
- Structural features (foreshadowing, dramatic irony, patterns, etc.)
- Word class (adjective, verb, abstract noun, adverb, etc.)
- Links to theme/context
- Synonyms

Why should I write down synonyms?

Synonyms are words or phrases that mean the same, or nearly the same, as other words or phrases. A common weakness I see in students' writing is using the same word in their analysis as the key word itself.

This usually looks something like:

> Orwell presents Snowball as a character who inspires the other animals to listen to him. This can be seen in the statement 'it was Snowball who was best at writing'. The use of the word 'best' highlights that out of all the animals Snowball is the <u>best writer</u> and this is why he ends up teaching the other animals – except the pigs – how to <u>write</u>.

If a student can use good synonyms for the words on which they are focusing, their analysis is likely to be more impressive:

> Orwell presents Snowball as a character who inspires the other animals to listen to him. This can be seen in the statement 'it was Snowball who was best at writing'. The use of the word 'best' highlights that out of all the animals Snowball is the <u>most impressive writer</u> and this is why he ends up teaching the other animals – except the pigs – how to <u>put pen to paper</u>.

Being careful about when we use the word 'quote'

Quote is a word we use for evidence taken from a text to support our analysis. Writers don't use quotes – readers do! So, it sounds clumsy and unsophisticated when we write things like:

> *Austen's use of the* quote *'She is tolerable; but not handsome enough to tempt me' is important as it gives the reader a sense of Darcy's poor manners and sense of social superiority.*

This isn't right: Austen hasn't written or used a 'quote'. We have! For that reason, we should only use the word 'quote' when we're discussing evidence we'll use in our essay. But we shouldn't use the actual word in our own analytical writing.

How can we avoid it? Ways to replace the word 'quote' in your essay include:

✔ **Use the word 'phrase', 'line' or 'dialogue' instead:**
Austen's use of the line 'She is tolerable; but not handsome enough to tempt me' is important…

✔ **Identify language feature (if there is one):** Austen's use of irony in 'It is a truth universally acknowledged, that a single man in possession of a good fortune, must be in want of a wife' implies…

✔ **Identify sentence function:** Austen's use of the exclamatory 'How despicably I have acted!' is important…

Choosing your synonyms carefully

Many words have lots of synonyms, but some of these synonyms are usually far more suitable than others. Synonyms for the word 'friend', for example, include the words mate, pal, buddy. So if I was intending to use the quote 'Whatever goes upon four legs, or has wings, is a friend' from *Animal Farm*, I might write down these words as potential synonyms that I could use when analysing the quote.

But these words are too colloquial to be used in an essay. **Colloquial language** is informal language, such as slang, that we might use in everyday conversation. Good academic writing, however, requires more formal language. A much more impressive list of synonyms for friend would include: acquaintance, associate, companion.

If you struggle to think of more ambitious synonyms off the top of your head, you can solve this problem by using a thesaurus. And even if you're someone who has got an excellent vocabulary, your analysis will still benefit from a few juicy synonyms. If you haven't got a copy of a thesaurus at home, you can use an online one. Either way is fine. You do need to be careful, however, if you come across a word you've never heard of. It may be similar to the word you're analysing, but it might not work in the context in which you're using it. If in doubt, make sure you use a dictionary to double check the meaning.

Compiling a list of effective synonyms

Let's take another look at the synonyms I've used in my exploded quote about Snowball from *Animal Farm*:

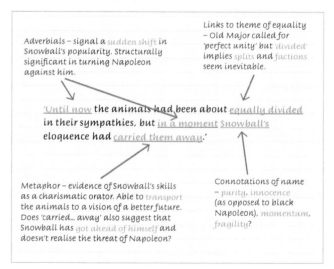

Key word/phrase	Synonym(s)
until now, in a moment	sudden shift
divided	splits, factions
carried… away	transport, got ahead of himself
Snowball	purity, innocence, momentum, fragility

Looking through a thesaurus, I can see that I could have possibly added the following:

Key word/phrase	Synonym(s)
until now	**up to this point**, **previously**, formerly
divided	**separated**, **torn apart**, severed
carried... away	**captivated**, seduced, **spellbound**
Snowball	projectile

Certain synonyms on my list (highlighted in bold) work really well, so will be added to my exploded quote plan. Hopefully, you can see that a bit of extra work finding impressive vocabulary will really help improve my analysis.

Synonyms – a vital ingredient for effective analysis

✔ Prepare the words you're going to use in advance.

✔ Reduces the chance of you repeating the key word in your analysis.

✔ Helps you learn and use impressive vocabulary.

✔ Use a thesaurus when you get stuck, or for really ambitious words.

If you prefer, you could make your own exploding quotes sheet to use. Here's an example of what these might look like:

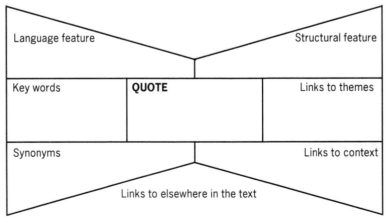

Whether you prefer to use a sheet of A4 to roughly explode your quotes or a template with separate categories is totally up to you. Try both formats and see which best suits your thinking.

Creating exploded quote flashcards

Once you've built up a bank of exploded quotes, you're ready for the next step. You need to ensure that you can remember all the clever things you're going to write about your key quotes. For that, you need to add exploded quotes to your stack of flashcards. Then you can make them part of your daily retrieval practice routine.

Here's an example flashcard, featuring an exploded quote from *A Christmas Carol*:

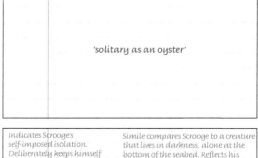

Look closely at the card and you'll see it includes the following:
- Language feature – clear explanation of the precise effect of the simile 'solitary as an oyster'.
- Key words – detailed focus on 'solitary' and 'oyster'.
- Structural features – links to description of Scrooge as 'clutching', building up a pattern of his closed personality.
- Synonyms – solitary = isolated, aloof, avoiding contact; oyster = hard exterior, reluctant to open up, clutching, unwelcoming, goodness within.

It may be improved, however, by including:

- word class (adjective, verb, abstract noun, adverb, etc.)
- links to theme/context
- analytical verbs

What are analytical verbs?

Analytical verbs are verbs that you use in your written analysis of texts. These verbs help make it clear what you think a writer is doing and why:

> In 'When We Two Parted', Byron uses the diction 'silence' to indicate the distance that can grow between two former lovers as a relationship ends. The noun is ambiguous, however, as it could also imply a layer of secrecy associated with an illicit love affair.

Other useful analytical verbs that you could include as part of your planned analysis include:

Amplifies	emphasises by adding extra impact
Conveys	gets across a message/idea/theory
Demonstrates	provides a clear explanation/example
Emphasises	draws attention to something
Evokes	brings about a strong feeling or idea
Foreshadows	hints at subsequent events/themes
Highlights	draws clear attention to make it stand out
Reiterates	repeats or supports the same point/idea
Reveals	makes clear something previously unclear
Symbolises	uses something to represent an idea or theme

Putting it all together

Having a bank of these exploded quotes makes it much easier when you move on to writing detailed practice paragraphs as part of your revision. Knowing what you're going to write about key quotes will allow you to spend more time in the exam getting your excellent ideas on paper, and less time scratching your head thinking about what you're going to focus on, and thinking about why you picked this quote in the first place.

66 Top 5 to thrive

1. Practise exploding quotes to make sure you can analyse each quote in detail.

2. Make sure you include interesting synonyms for the key words in each quote.

3. Use a thesaurus to help with ambitious words, but double check the meaning.

4. Transfer your exploded quotes to flashcards and make them part of your retrieval practice.

5. Make sure you include developed notes about language and structure, and make links to themes and context.

Building up a bank of 'killer quotes'

Knowing long lists of quotes is great. Being able to remember who said what, what happened when, and which words link to which themes will leave you feeling confident as you enter your English literature exams.

But while all quotes are important, some are far more important than others. If you select your quotes really carefully, you'll find that you won't necessarily need a massive list of quotes to choose from. If you can identify and understand 'killer quotes' for each text, you'll find that they can cover pretty much everything.

What does 'killer quote' mean?

Killer quotes are memorable, powerful and – most importantly – very versatile. Things that are versatile can be used for many different jobs. Killer quotes are able to cover most key themes. Often, they also help us understand the main characters. Usually, they illustrate important ideas about context as well. The word 'killer' isn't anything to do with murder. In this case, it is a slang term that means 'exceptional', 'amazing' or 'effective'. So, killer quotes are the ones that stand out as the most useful. They're the ones that can help you out with even the trickiest exam questions. Think a Swiss Army knife, but with brilliant ideas instead of a saw, screwdriver and a tin opener!

Killer quotes – multipurpose quotes for all situations

✔ They're short and easy to remember.

✔ The powerful language allows you to plan impressive analysis.

✔ Structurally significant, they provide lots of links to the rest of the text.

✔ They cover most of the themes so can be used in virtually any exam question.

How can I identify killer quotes?

Here is my five-step guide to spotting quotes that can be used for most exam questions you're likely to encounter:

1. Re-read the texts and look out for quotes that grab your attention

You may have missed out on particularly significant quotes the first or second time you read the book. Read it again with fresh eyes. There may well be new and important extracts that catch your attention.

2. Look back through your notes from class

Are there any particular quotes that your English teachers spent ages going over, exploding on the board, linking to different bits of context and other parts of the text? If so, there's a good chance that your teacher thinks that it's an important one. Discuss this with your friends and your teacher. Are there certain ones that you all end up coming back to?

3. Scan through your list of quotes for the key themes from each text

Do some of them crop up repeatedly? Might they be used as well as, or instead of, some of your other choices? If they seem to fit most things, they may well be killer quote candidates.

4. Test out potential killer quotes

Take a quote that you think fits the killer quote category, and tick it off against each theme. Also, consider how it might link to important context. If you've got lots of ticks, you're in business. If not, then it may be a decent quote to use, but it's not killer material!

Check out my example from *An Inspector Calls*:

Mr Birling: 'unsinkable, absolutely unsinkable'	
Key theme	**Good example?**
Social responsibility	✗
Wealth and power	✓
Guilt and blame	✗
Gender inequality	✗
Generational differences	✓

I'm a big fan of '…unsinkable, absolutely unsinkable' because it's such a useful quote for looking at Priestley's portrayal of Birling as an arrogant and ignorant character, who embodies the complacent selfishness of the capitalist system. It's a lovely example of dramatic irony and helps us understand how the 1940s audience are meant to respond to the head of the family. But after having matched it against the key themes, like the *Titanic*, it doesn't quite stay afloat.

Going through your quotes like this is a really useful exercise. Even when you're ruling out possible killer quotes, you're revising your understanding of the quotes and the themes.

5. Check that they match up with other key quotes

One sure sign of a brilliant killer quote is that it pairs up nicely with other important quotes from the text. Sometimes, it fits with several quotes on the same focus. When this happens, you can more easily spot patterns throughout the structure of the texts. This allows you to write about similarities, contrasts or motifs that run through the text as a whole. By doing this, you'll cover structure as well as language, which is really important.

Let's have a look at the following example from *Lord of the Flies*:

● **'He swung back his right arm and hurled the spear with all his strength'**

This killer quote covers many of the central themes, including civilisation and savagery, power, innocence and loss of innocence and identity.

Now notice how it links beautifully with:

● 'The madness came into his eyes again.
"I thought I might kill."'

And this:

● 'Jack spoke loudly.
"This head is for the beast. It's a gift."'

Then finally:

● 'He pushed his hair up and gazed at the green and black mask before him, trying to remember what Jack looked like.'

Starting with the image of Jack as the primitive hunter figure, we can track the motif of strength, violence and savagery through the three quotes that follow. The first highlights Jack's increasing bloodthirstiness. The second illustrates how Jack, with his sacrificial kill, worships the beast in a way that reminds us of our primitive ancestors. The third demonstrates how Jack's identity becomes increasingly blurred and inhuman as he moves further away from the values of civilisation.

Practise doing this with possible killer quotes from the texts that you study. The more links you can make, the more likely they are to be the most useful quotes for your exam.

I still can't find killer quotes. Help!

If you've followed my steps but are still struggling to identify the most helpful quotes, then don't worry. Using some detailed examples from expert English teachers, I'm going to give you a list of very important quotes from the most popular texts that are studied for GCSE English literature. I'm not saying these are the only quotes you need to learn. And I'm not saying you shouldn't build up your own preferred list of quotes. But if you're stuck – or are looking for essential quotes to develop your selection – then this is definitely a good place to start.

Shakespeare

Macbeth – killer quotes

1. **'fair is foul, and foul is fair' (Act 1, Scene 1, line 12)**

   - Sets up the paradox that runs throughout the play: appearances don't always match with reality.
   - Note the alliteration and reversed structure of this phrase – a language feature known as chiasmus.
   - These emphasise the grey areas of morality in the play. While the Witches might think it's fair to murder to become king, others might consider it foul.
   - Links to: 'So foul and fair a day I have not seen'; 'I... begin to doubt the equivocation of the fiend that lies like truth...'.

2. **'full of scorpions is my mind' (Act 3, Scene 2, line 36)**
   - Exemplifies the central idea of the play: unchecked ambition leading to tragic consequences.
   - In this metaphor, Shakespeare uses the animal imagery of the scorpion to represent Macbeth's conscience. He's attacked and stung by constant feelings of guilt.
   - Links to: 'Be lion-mettled, proud, and take no care'.

3. **'look like the innocent flower/But be the serpent under't' (Act 1, Scene 5, lines 74–75)**

   This is English teacher Rebecca Lowman's favourite killer quote. She explains why it's so versatile:

   - Covering most of the key themes, including violence and loyalty, it portrays Lady Macbeth as an unconventional 11th century wife. It also depicts the power imbalance between the couple.

- Includes fascinating language such as:
  - Imperatives: 'Look... be' – the commands reinforce the idea of Lady Macbeth being in control.
  - Simile: 'like' – using the pastoral imagery of the flower implies she wants Macbeth to appear gentle and pleasant on the surface.
  - Metaphor, contrast and Biblical allusion: 'serpent' – but in reality she wants him to be motivated by evil, Satanic intent.
- Relates to the medal commissioned by James I to celebrate the discovery of the Gunpowder Plot.
- Structurally significant – her manipulation clearly works, as not long after Macbeth says 'False face must hide what the false heart doth know'.
- Links to: 'When the battle's won and lost'.

4. **'will all great Neptune's ocean wash this blood clean from my hand?' (Act 2, Scene 2, lines 78–79)**
- The rhetorical question sums up Macbeth's reflective and conflicted character.
- Referring to Neptune, ruler of all the vast oceans, exaggerates the amount of water Macbeth believes is required to cleanse his hands of blood.
- The single-word motif 'blood' is used over 40 times in the play, symbolising violence and guilt.
- Links to: 'A little water will clear us of this deed'; 'out, damned spot'; 'all the perfumes of Arabia will not sweeten this little hand'.

5. **'strange things I have in head, that will to hand' (Act 3, Scene 4, line 145)**

'The firstlings of my heart shall be the firstlings of my hand.' (Act 4, Scene 1, lines 63–64)

According to English teacher Matt Lynch, this pair of quotes best helps us understand Macbeth's character development:
- Both end with the image of the hand, signifying action.
- Traditionally, the head is usually seen as the source of wisdom, while the heart is the place from where emotion comes.
- Initially, Macbeth attempts to separate his thoughts from his actions.
- Yet, later he abandons rational thought entirely, admitting that he'll be driven by impulse and emotion to preserve his life and throne.

Romeo and Juliet – killer quotes

1. **'These violent delights have violent ends' (Act 2, Scene 6, line 9)**
   - Friar Lawrence's warning acts as the play's neat central message: avoid extreme emotions, especially love that is excessive.
   - Contrast of 'delights' and 'ends' fits the key theme of the opposition of love and hate, as well as fate, relationships, honour and violence.
   - Ironically, the Friar doesn't heed his own warning and rushes into plans to keep the two lovers together, with dire consequences.
   - Links to: 'love moderately'; 'they stumble that run fast'; 'More light and light, more dark and dark our woes!'; 'See what a scourge is laid upon your hate/That heaven finds means to kill your joys with love'.

2. **'O, I am fortune's fool!' (Act 3, Scene 1, line 98)**
   - After killing Tybalt, Romeo suddenly realises the unavoidable consequences of his reckless behaviour.
   - The alliteration and personification tie together his impulsive behaviour and the inevitability of his tragic fate. Because of his actions, fate now has control of his destiny.
   - Links to: 'a pair of star-crossed lovers'; 'From forth the fatal loins of these two foes'; 'A greater power than we can contradict/Hath thwarted our intents'.

3. **'This intrusion shall/Now seeming sweet, convert to bitterest gall' (Act 1, Scene 5, lines 90–91)**
   - The inciting incident (event that begins the problem of the story) highlights how Tybalt is determined to continue the 'ancient grudge' between the two families.
   - He sees the 'intrusion' as an insult to his family's honour.
   - The superlative 'bitterest' indicates that Tybalt is driven by hate, in contrast to the sweetness of the lovers.
   - Links to: 'the mad blood stirring'; 'fire-ey'd fury be my conduct now'.

4. **'O, she doth teach the torches to burn bright' (Act 1, Scene 5, line 42)**
   - Fusion of hyperbole and alliteration evoke the sheer force of Romeo's – soon to be mutual – attraction to Juliet.

- Their feelings of love, and lust, are passionate and intense. But, like the metaphorical torch, their love is destined to consume itself and become extinguished.
- Links to: 'Juliet is the sun'; 'Young men's love then lies… in their eyes'; 'I have bought the mansion of a love/But not possess'd it'; 'This is thy sheath; there rust and let me die'.

5. **'A plague o' both your houses' (Act 3, Scene 1, line 59)**
    - Mercutio has been a loyal friend to Romeo, but has paid for it with his life.
    - As a relative of the Prince and Paris, he is trapped between the warring families.
    - His repeated metaphorical curse predicts the suffering that both households must endure with the loss of their children.
    - Links to: 'Peace, I hate the word'; 'my fingers itch'; 'Do with their death, bury their parents' strife'.

Much Ado About Nothing – killer quotes

1. **'Thou and I are too wise to woo peaceably' (Act 5, Scene 2, line 54)**

2. **'Peace, I will stop your mouth' (Act 5, Scene 4, line 96)**

3. **'I know you of old' (Act 1, Scene 1, line 114)**

4. **'But fare thee well, most foul, most fair, farewell/Thou pure impiety and impious purity' (Act 4, Scene 1, lines 104–105)**

5. **'Hath Leonato any son, my lord?' 'No child but Hero; she's his only heir' (Act 1, Scene 1, lines 232–233)**

The Merchant of Venice – killer quotes

1. **'I would not have given it for a wilderness of monkeys' (Act 3, Scene 1, line 103)**

2. **'The villainy you teach me I will execute' (Act 3, Scene 1, line 72)**

3. **'The quality of mercy is not strained; It droppeth as the gentle rain from heaven/Upon the place beneath.' (Act 4, Scene 1, lines 173–175)**

4. **'All that glisters is not gold' (Act 2, Scene 7, line 69)**

5. **'If you prick us do we not bleed?' (Act 3, Scene 1, line 65)**

19th century novels

A Christmas Carol – killer quotes

1. **'as solitary as an oyster' (Stave 1)**
   - The simile depicts Scrooge's self-imposed isolation and tough, cold exterior.
   - Links to: 'Hard and sharp as a flint'; 'as merry as a schoolboy'.

2. **'mankind was my business' (Stave 1)**
   - Marley's ghost acts here as a mouthpiece for Dickens' beliefs. Kindness and humanity over profit and exploitation.
   - Links to: 'decrease the surplus population'.

3. **'fellow-passengers to the grave' (Stave 1)**
   - Fred's metaphorical comment illustrates that death is inevitable for us all yet makes clear that we still have the opportunity to shape the meaning of our lives.

4. **'I wear the chain I forged in life' (Stave 1)**
   - The chain is symbolic of Marley's guilt. A burden made from links that accumulated throughout his time on Earth.
   - The dynamic verb 'forged' is significant – Marley recognises that he actively created his guilt. This was a choice made of his own free will.
   - The links of the chain also symbolise how we are bound together as a society.

5. **'The mention of his name cast a dark shadow' (Stave 3)**
   - Shadows act as a motif throughout the novella:
     - They are associated with ghosts and premonitions – 'Are these the shadows of the things that Will be...?'
     - London's slums, and the people who live there, are dismal and 'shadowy'.
   - Significantly, these shadows lift at the end. See how Scrooge finds himself in the 'cheerful' lighting of the Cratchits' house and the 'golden sunlight' outside.

Jekyll and Hyde – killer quotes

1. **'I have been doomed to such a dreadful shipwreck' (Chapter 10)**
   - The metaphorical shipwreck is symbolic of not only the end of Jekyll's life but also his destroyed reputation.

- 'doomed' indicates the inevitability of this happening in a society that forces people to repress their true selves.
- Forms a motif of broken wood, which is linked to duality: the 'splintered' cane, 'the wreck of the door' as Utterson and Poole force entry to Jekyll's laboratory.
- Links to: 'concealed my pleasures'.

2. **'man is not truly one, but truly two' (Chapter 10)**
   - The repetition of 'truly' illustrates the primitive side of human nature that lurks within us all.
   - Links to: 'polar twins'; 'commingled out of good and evil'; 'a solution of the bonds of obligation'.

3. **'ape-like fury' (Chapter 4)**
   - The simile places the 'troglodytic' Hyde in the context of Darwin's theory of evolution. His depraved behaviour is compared to our savage ancestors.
   - Links to: 'trampled calmly'; 'like a damned juggernaut'.

4. **'my devil had been caged, he came out roaring' (Chapter 10)**
   - Uses the Gothic trope of Satanic behaviour to amplify the sense of evil within Jekyll.
   - The metaphor of imprisonment and escape highlights the consequences of repressed forbidden desire.
   - Links to: 'like a disconsolate prisoner'.

5. **'transcendental medicine' (Chapter 9)**
   - Acts as an oxymoron – 'medicine' is based on the empirical methods of science, whereas 'transcendental' relates to the mystical and spiritual world.
   - The contradiction emphasises Jekyll's successful but disastrous attempts to combine the power of science and the supernatural.
   - Links to: 'unscientific balderdash'.

The Sign of Four – killer quotes

1. **'You really are an automaton – a calculating machine!' (Chapter 2)**
2. **'He leaned forward in his chair with an expression of extraordinary concentration upon his clear-cut, hawk-like features' (Chapter 2)**

3. 'Whoever had lost a treasure, I knew that night that I had gained one.' **(Chapter 12)**

4. 'To him it brought murder, to Major Sholto it brought fear and guilt, to me it has meant slavery for life' **(Chapter 11)**

5. 'Eliminate all other factors, and the one which remains must be the truth.' **(Chapter 1)**

Modern texts

An Inspector Calls – killer quotes

1. 'We are members of one body' **(Act 3)**
   - An urgent call for socialism. The first-person plural pronoun 'we' emphasises the need for collective responsibility.
   - Links to: 'like bees in a hive – community and all that nonsense'; 'There are millions and millions of John Smiths and Eva Smiths'.

2. 'they will be taught it in fire and blood and anguish' **(Act 3)**
   - Uses dramatic irony to allude to the world wars on the horizon.
   - 'Fire' also implies a Hellish outcome for the immoral members of society.
   - 'Blood' may also hint at the prospect of a socialist revolution if a capitalist society fails to curb its excesses.
   - Links to: 'A chain of events'; 'I can't accept any responsibility'.

3. 'I don't play golf' **(Act 1)**
   - Despite the dry humour, the Inspector's comment reveals his willingness to stand up to his social superiors.
   - Distancing him from the corrupt establishment at the top of the police force, it also emphasises his difference from 'normal' police officers.

4. 'impertinent' **(Act 2)**
   - Adjective meaning lacking respect for someone of a higher status.
   - Sheila gets Eva fired from Milward's by accusing her of being 'very impertinent'.
   - Yet Sheila laughs at her mother's use of the word to describe the Inspector, calling it a 'silly word'.

- Mr and Mrs Birling see themselves as socially superior. Even Sheila, who seems in opposition to her parents, sees it as a word that shouldn't be used. In other words, social hierarchy is obvious and doesn't need pointing out.

5. **'I must think' (Act 3)**
   - Sheila acts as the family's moral compass. As the others try to avoid responsibility, she accepts it.
   - Her rejection of Gerald mirrors her independent thought, highlighting gender, as well as social, conflict.
   - Links to: 'these girls aren't cheap labour, they're people'; 'it frightens me, the way you talk'.

Animal Farm – killer quotes

1. **'The creatures outside looked from pig to man, and from man to pig, and from pig to man again; but already it was impossible to say which was which.' (Chapter 10)**

2. **'All habits of man are evil. And, above all, no animal must ever tyrannise over his own' (Chapter 1)**

3. **'All that year, the animals worked like slaves' (Chapter 6)**

4. **'Never mind the milk comrades!' (Chapter 2)**

5. **'at the word "Snowball" all the dogs let out blood-curdling growls and showed their side teeth' (Chapter 7)**

Blood Brothers – killer quotes

1. **'he was about to commit a serious crime, love' and 'it was more of a prank, really' (Act 1)**

2. **'And do we blame superstition for what came to pass?' (Act 2)**

3. **'The devil's got your number' (Act 2)**

4. **'Just like Marilyn Monroe' (Acts 1 & 2)**

5. **'I could have been him!' (Act 2)**

Lord of the Flies – killer quotes

1. 'maybe there is a beast... maybe it's only us.' **(Chapter 5)**
2. 'Ralph wept for the end of innocence, the darkness of man's heart, and the fall through the air of a true, wise friend called Piggy.' **(Chapter 12)**
3. 'He swung back his right arm and hurled the spear with all his strength' **(Chapter 3)**
4. 'This head is for the beast. It's a gift.' **(Chapter 8)**
5. 'The water rose farther and dressed Simon's coarse hair with brightness.' **(Chapter 9)**

DNA – killer quotes

1. 'Chimps are evil' **(Act 1)**
2. 'Suddenly she stops chewing and spits the sweet out' **(Act 3)**
3. 'I'm going to have to... bite their face. Or something' **(Act 1)**
4. 'What's more important; one person or everyone?' **(Act 3)**
5. 'I threatened to gouge one of his eyes out' **(Act 3)**

66 Top 5 to thrive

1. Killer quotes are important because they're the most versatile.
2. Spend time identifying these quotes from your quote lists.
3. Make sure these quotes cover structure as well as language.
4. If you're stuck, use the killer quotes listed above.
5. Link killer quotes to other key quotes on the same theme for maximum effect.

99

Using context successfully

At various points in the literature exams, you will be expected to write about context. Different exam boards have different ways of focusing on context in the mark scheme. But one thing's for sure: it's hard to write a decent response about a book or poem that you've studied without knowing anything about who wrote it, when they wrote it, and why they wrote it.

So, context matters.

And for that reason, you'll hear your English teacher talk about it lots. Yet you might not fully understand what they mean by this vague term.

What exactly is 'context'?

In simple terms, context is the background to the text that you're studying. Typically, when we talk about the context of a novel, play or poem we often focus on things like:

- When the text was written.
- The importance of the setting.
- What society was like at that time (historical events, attitudes to religion and science, political movements, gender relations etc.).
- The writer's background and influences.
- How other writers from the genre may have affected the writing of the text.
- The significance of the writer's other works.
- For plays, how different versions have been performed.

Coping with context

Reading that list, you're probably thinking that's a lot of background information! If so, you're not alone.

My students often struggle with applying context. Particularly when it comes to older texts, like Shakespeare. Written over 400 years ago, there are so many different interpretations about what was going on at the time, and what Shakespeare was trying to say. No wonder my students aren't always sure what to include, and how to include it.

But don't worry. After I've shown them how to use context, they soon get better at applying it to their answers.

And, in this chapter, I'm going to show you how to make sure you use context appropriately and effectively, as part of your revision schedule. I'll explain how being selective in the context that you use will help you to write about it in a way that is clear, thoughtful and, crucially, relevant to the question.

Where most students go wrong with context

When it comes to context, there's a fine line between too little and too much. If you don't understand important background information, you won't really understand the text.

But if you write too much about background, you can drift away from the text itself, and fail to answer the question properly. Based on my experience, and exam board feedback, here's what can go wrong when it comes to context:

Writing about context: 7 common mistakes to avoid

✗ Not including any context.

✗ Too much context.

✗ Mixing up historical events or periods.

✗ Vague references to the past.

✗ Missing opportunities to write about genre or themes.

✗ Generalisations and simplifications.

✗ 'Bolt-on' context that isn't linked to themes, language or the question.

For each of these common context mistakes, I'll give you an example of what this might look like. Then I'll show you how you can work to overcome these problems during revision.

1. Not including any context

Imagine you get the following exam question: How does Priestley explore the importance of social class in *An Inspector Calls*?

There are plenty of opportunities to look at the relationships between characters of different class backgrounds. But it would be really difficult to answer this question successfully without making some reference to the social tensions of Britain before World War 1 (when the play is set), or the changing political landscape of Britain just after World War 2 (when the play was first performed).

Solution – If you find yourself with big context gaps in your essays, go back to your exploded quotes and add relevant context on your flashcards. Use your class notes if necessary.

For example, Mr Birling's dialogue 'If you don't come down sharply on some of these people' relates to the trade unions, who by 1912 were beginning to campaign for better wages, upsetting capitalist factory owners like Birling.

2. Too much context

But you also need to remember that you are studying for a literature exam, not a history exam. For that reason, context needs to be selective. On that type of question, contextual details might only make up 20% of the marks. So, an answer that spends all its time focusing on the struggle for socialism in Edwardian Britain isn't going to do well.

Solution – Look carefully at the balance of the paragraphs you write as part of your revision. You'll still need to spend most of your time looking at the presentation of key characters and themes, as well as analysing language, such as the adverb 'sharply' from the quote above.

3. Mixing up historical events or periods

I've lost count of the number of times I've seen Dr Jekyll and Scrooge described as characters from the Elizabethan era. Or have read about a Victorian audience's response to Juliet or Shylock.

Mistakes can happen in exams, but I often get the sense that this is a revision issue. Students get mixed up because they struggle to understand the difference between historical periods, seeing literary texts as all coming from the distant past.

Solution – If you struggle with remembering key periods, make yourself a timeline, which can be added to your retrieval practice. In this example, a student who is studying *Macbeth*, *A Christmas Carol*, AQA's *Love and Relationships* poetry anthology and *Blood Brothers* has started mapping out key dates and periods:

1606	1816	1843	1867	1983
(Jacobean period) *Macbeth*	(Romanticism) 'When We Two Parted'	(Victorian period) *A Christmas Carol*	(Victorian period) 'Neutral Tones'	(Thatcherism) *Blood Brothers*

4. Vague references to the past

In exams, students often write things like 'in those days' or 'at that time'. Statements like this sound vague and unconfident about dates and historical periods. With some texts, however, the background context is too complex to just link to a certain publication date. Take *Macbeth* for example. It was probably first performed in the summer of 1606. It celebrates the reign of James I who became King of England in 1603. But it is set in 11th century Scotland.

Some poems about World War 1, such as Wilfred Owen's 'Exposure', were written during the war based on the poet's experience. Others, like Ted Hughes' 'Bayonet Charge' (1957) – which uses a persona to imagine what trench warfare must have been like – were published many years later.

Solution – Practise writing sentences that make it clear which period you're referring to. Ensure your timeline reflects the more complicated historical context of some texts.

5. Missing opportunities to write about genre or recurring themes

Students often believe that context is just about what was going on when the book was written, or is set. But, as the list at the start of this chapter shows, there's far more to it than that. Done well, writing about genre or recurring themes is a really good way to place the text you're studying into a wider context.

Solution – Dedicate part of your revision schedule to learning about genre, then practising applying these ideas to your analysis of exploded quotes.

For example, if you're studying a Gothic text, like *Jekyll and Hyde*, *Frankenstein* or *Jane Eyre*, you should spend some of your revision time looking at how your text uses Gothic tropes. A trope is a common idea or motif that crops up repeatedly in a particular genre.

This student's example is from *Jekyll and Hyde*:

Gothic trope	Example from text
Isolation and imprisonment	'like a disconsolate prisoner'
The Satanic	'it was hellish to see'
Crisis	'ape-like fury'
The supernatural	'his face came suddenly black and the features seemed to melt and alter'
Sex and sexuality	'I concealed my pleasures'

But what might this look like as a practice paragraph?

> Stevenson uses the simile 'like a disconsolate prisoner' to show how Jekyll is forced into self-isolation in an attempt to repress his true desires. The adjective 'disconsolate' highlights how this seclusion causes Jekyll to feel dejected and hopeless. Stevenson employs the Gothic trope of imprisonment and isolation but adapts it to fit the context of Victorian society. In Gothic texts, characters are usually imprisoned against their will but Jekyll is presented as a self-enforced 'prisoner', trying to ward off the urges that come from within.

The impressive thing about the practice paragraph above is that it goes beyond just identifying the Gothic trope used by Stevenson. It makes sure that it links the trope to Stevenson's language and the specific themes of the novel.

6. Generalisations and simplifications

Students often take a general idea about the past and end up making sweeping statements about everyone from that era. They overgeneralise by writing things like 'everyone was religious in the Victorian period' or 'A 17th-century audience would feel shocked by...' or 'working-class people are all...'

A classic example I see when reading *Romeo and Juliet* essays is the idea that, in Shakespeare's time, daughters had no say over who they were to marry. This leads students to write things like:

> It was normal for girls to get married at 13.
> In the patriarchal Elizabethan period, as
> the head of the household, fathers made all
> the decisions on behalf of their children.

There are a couple of things wrong with this:

- Early marriage for girls was more common among noble families than the poor. But even for richer families, it wasn't the norm.
- The Medieval Church expected parents to take their children's view about potential marriages into consideration. For example, in Act 1, Scene 2, Lord Capulet tells Paris 'An she agreed within her scope of choice/Lies my consent and fair according voice'. In other words, *if Juliet agrees to marry you, you will have my blessing.*

Solution – Make sure your statements are carefully phrased. Don't assume that people from a particular time all acted and thought alike! Head of English Chris Curtis recommends the following tips to help you be more precise about context:

- Relate your analysis to the rules of the time:
  - What were the social rules governing men?
  - What were the rules for the poor?
  - What was the general attitude towards the rich?
- Think of things in terms of power:
  - Who had power at that time?
  - Who had no power?

Also, remember that characters are fictional and are often extreme examples, created for the purpose of narrative conflict. Practise writing paragraphs that take these ideas into account:

> The use of the ultimatum 'or I will drag thee on a hurdle thither' indicates Capulet's fury at his daughter's defiance. A 'hurdle' was used in Elizabethan times to transport dead bodies to the morgue, which emphasises Capulet's anger by suggesting that he would rather see her dead than refuse the marriage. It's important to remember that the Medieval Church asked parents to consider their children's view about possible marriages. Therefore, members of Shakespeare's audience may well see Capulet's threatening use of the dynamic verb 'drag' as an unacceptable overreaction, even in a patriarchal society where men were the heads of the household.

7.   'Bolt-on' context that isn't linked to themes, language or the question

As far as examiners are concerned, this is the most common context mistake of all. But what do we mean by 'bolt-on'? When we make a machine, we screw on different parts, bolting separate bits on as we go. When students use 'bolt-on' context, it means that they are adding it on at the end, without carefully linking it to themes, language or the question. Paragraphs in English aren't machines! They need all the elements to be woven together like a wooden basket, rather than sticking separate sections on at the end.

Here's an example paragraph of bolt-on context, with an explanation of what's gone wrong:

This part of the paragraph works well: the analysis of language is clear and successfully explains the writer's methods. ✓	In 'London', the writer's repetition of the phrase 'In every' indicates that poverty and misery are widespread. Through this, Blake highlights how hardship is universal and affects young and old.
This part is bolt-on context. The biographical information is correct, but the ideas don't fit with the language and themes in the opening part. ✗	Blake had an intense dislike of organised religion. For Blake, the true God was the power of human imagination.

As part of your revision, you need to work on making sure your context fits with the other parts of your analysis. If in doubt, ask your teacher.

So what might a good example of this look like?

The content is directly relevant to the original point and the analysis of language. ✓	In 'London', Blake's phrase 'Every blackning church appalls' uses each 'church' the speaker passes as a symbol of the uncaring nature of the religious establishment. Through the metaphorical verb 'blackning', Blake suggests that the Church is partly responsible for the dark and miserable lives of the young chimney sweeps.
The student develops the context, then links back to the quote. This makes sure the information about Blake's beliefs is fully integrated. ✓	Despite his strong belief in the Bible, Blake had an intense dislike of organised religion. For Blake, the Church of England was a hypocritical institution. It possessed great wealth but did little to protect the children forced into dangerous work. By linking the 'appalling' soot-stained churches with the woeful chimney sweeps, Blake shows his disgust at the clergy's lack of action on child poverty.

Still not sure? Let's take another look at an example of how context and analysis should be weaved together, rather than bolted on:

This example starts with relevant context, rather than bolting it on at the end. ✓	James I was obsessed with the power of witchcraft, writing *Daemonologie* in 1597 to showcase his expertise on the subject. Through his portrayal of the Witches, Shakespeare appeals to the King's fascination with the supernatural. On a surface level, the use of the metaphor 'Though you untie the winds' illustrates Macbeth's willingness to involve himself with malevolent beings in order to gain the crown. The verb phrase 'untie the winds' indicates the Witches' power by showing how they can exert unnatural control over the elements. There is little doubt that James would have been deeply affected by this particular language. In 1589, a violent storm nearly killed James and his new bride. He believed that witchcraft was used in a deliberate attempt to kill him. On a deeper level, therefore, Shakespeare uses 'untie' to emphasise the presence of evil forces who can unleash chaos and try to commit regicide.
The student develops the context and again specifically links it back to the close analysis of language. ✓	

66 Top 5 to thrive

1. As part of your revision, consider the different types of context you can use.

2. Think about what context will be relevant to which questions.

3. Make sure you have the right balance: avoid including too much or too little context.

4. Improve your knowledge of the time periods, and genre tropes, to avoid incorrect or vague statements.

5. Practise writing paragraphs – using my examples as a model – to ensure your context blends in smoothly with your analysis.

99

Improving practice essays

You've learnt the quotes. You've worked out which ones are the most important. You know what context fits best with which bits of analysis. You've practised writing paragraphs in class, and as part of your revision.

By now you're ready to tackle practice essay questions. Before you start writing these essays during revision, let's quickly remind ourselves of the ingredients of a good GCSE English essay:

- An effective introduction
- Main body – includes analysis of writer's methods
- A logical structure that answers the question
- Clear comparison (where necessary)
- A neat conclusion
- Well-written, with interesting ideas

In my experience, students understand why they need to practise writing responses to essay questions. Just like in Maths or Geography or Spanish, they know that having a go at previous exam questions will help them prepare for future ones. They struggle, however, with knowing how to revise for English essays. They know roughly what needs to go into an English essay. But they don't always know precisely how to practise these key ingredients.

So how can I revise these parts of an essay?

Before we look at the separate sections of an essay, there's one important thing I want to tell you about essays, revision and exams.

Students who do well in exams usually have a very clear idea about what they're going to write before they go into the exam!

This means they'll have done lots of practice writing parts of essays in revision. They'll have practised putting the best paragraphs together to form impressive full essays. They'll have practised tweaking these essays to fit other similar exam questions. And, most crucially, they'll have used retrieval practice to memorise the best chunks of their work.

One I made earlier – how to prepare quality essay responses

✓ Write practice paragraphs on your key quotes.

✓ Improve them during revision.

✓ Use your introduction as an essay plan.

✓ Practise getting your best paragraphs into essays.

✓ Spend time adapting these essays to fit other exam questions.

✓ Memorise the best parts of your essays.

Preparing essay introductions for novels and plays

Why are introductions such an important part of your revision? I usually find that students who struggle to write an effective introduction haven't planned out what they are going to write about. For this reason, their introductions are usually full of waffle.

The best introductions make complex points in a few sentences. They understand that writers create characters, not real people. They understand the key ideas and the bigger picture. They know what the writer was trying to say when they wrote the text.

Here's an example for a question about the theme of love and hate in *Romeo and Juliet*:

> In Romeo and Juliet, love that is driven by 'violent delights' has destructive power and leads to 'violent ends'. In blurring the boundary between love and hate, Shakespeare emphasises how both 'rancour' and 'boundless', excessive love destroys our rational thoughts. At the play's end, love does defeat hate, but it takes the tragic sacrifice of the naïve and impetuous 'star-crossed lovers' to heal a divided community.

This example gets across the following key ideas:
- Intense passion can be destructive.
- Love and hate overlap.
- Romeo and Juliet's youthful love is rushed and idealistic.
- It takes the tragic deaths of Romeo and Juliet to heal the feud.

This introduction can now be used as a rough plan for the rest of the essay. By matching these key ideas with your favourite quotes on the theme of love, you can logically move through the main body of your essay, making sure you properly answer the question.

What about other essay questions?

An important part of your revision is practising adapting the introduction for similar theme questions. For *Romeo and Juliet*, this might include:

- Relationships
- Marriage
- Strong feelings
- Violence
- Conflict

For example:

> In Romeo and Juliet, a marriage driven by 'violent delights', and based on destructive passion, leads to 'violent ends'. Shakespeare uses the union of the young lovers to blur the boundaries between love and hate, highlighting the consequences of the dangerous combination of 'rancour' and 'boundless', excessive love. At the play's end, the 'alliance' of Romeo and Juliet does defeat hate, but it takes the tragic sacrifice of the naïve and impetuous 'star-crossed lovers' to heal a divided community.

Let's take a look at another example, this time a question with a character focus, from *A Christmas Carol*:

> Portrayed as a selfish and mean-spirited character at the start of the novella, Scrooge represents the 'clutching' greed of the more privileged elements of Victorian Britain. In presenting Scrooge's desire to 'decrease the surplus population', Dickens critiques callous Malthusian ideas about poverty and social justice. At the end of the novel, however, Scrooge's moral transformation is used to symbolise the redemptive power of Christmas, and act as a reminder to society that 'mankind [is our] business'.

This example gets across the following key ideas about Scrooge:

- At the start, he symbolises the greed of the Victorian elite.
- Dickens uses his character to question ideas about population growth.
- Scrooge undergoes a significant change in the novella.
- The Ghosts' visits remind him of the importance of human interaction and kindness.

As with the *Romeo and Juliet* example, this introduction can act as a rough plan for the rest of the essay's paragraphs.

Notice how all of the examples I've given focus on the key word ('marriage', for example) from the questions in the introduction. As well as referring to it at the start, examiners will expect you to refer to the key word from the question throughout the full essay. When using my method of adapting prepared responses, it's really important that you do this, or you will lose marks!

Preparing essay introductions for poetry

An excellent way of showing you understand the main techniques and ideas in the poems is to prepare a brief introduction for each of the anthology poems that you study. I recommend that my students use this format:

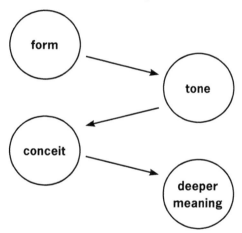

What do these terms mean?

Form is the type of poem. For example, an elegy is a type of poem written to remember someone who has died. A sonnet is a 14-line poem, traditionally written in iambic pentameter. A didactic poem instructs the reader and gives a clear moral message.

Tone is the writer's or speaker's attitude towards a subject. This is revealed through their point of view or choice of words.

Conceit is an extended metaphor that runs throughout the poem.

Deeper meaning is the poem's key ideas or themes. This is often hidden beneath what the poem seems to be about.

'My Last Duchess' by Robert Browning: an example introduction

> In 'My Last Duchess', Browning uses the <u>dramatic monologue form</u> to present the Duke as a powerful and disturbing individual who is determined to control the Duchess, even in death. The poet creates an <u>arrogant tone</u> to highlight the Duke's egotistical viewpoint. Through the <u>conceit of the painting that seems 'alive'</u> but is actually a lifeless possession, Browning reveals how male power has been traditionally used to dominate and silence free-spirited women, simultaneously reflecting hypocritical Victorian attitudes towards sin.

Deeper meaning

Using this structure, you can plan introductions for all of the poems that you study. Then, during revision, you can practise including comparison in these introductions by bringing in a second poem:

Comparing 'My Last Duchess' to 'Poppies' by Jane Weir: an example introduction

> In 'Poppies', Weir also uses the <u>dramatic monologue form</u> to explore attitudes about control. Yet, by contrast, the maternal persona in 'Poppies' is portrayed as hopeful, anxious and lacking in power, now that her son has asserted his independence and left for war. Unlike in 'My Last Duchess', the poet creates a <u>melancholic tone</u> to illustrate the mother's nostalgic desire to protect her son like when he was younger. Through <u>the conceit of the uniformed young soldier</u>, impatient to prove himself on the battlefield, Weir reveals the mother's inability to stop him growing up. Here, we see a different kind of destructive male power to the Duke's: the 'intoxicating' masculine ideal of the glory of dying for one's country.

Deeper meaning

Preparing the main body of your essay

Here's an example question for the play *DNA* by Dennis Kelly:

How does Kelly present ideas about morality in *DNA*?

As part of their revision, a student has written a practice paragraph, using one of the killer quotes from Chapter 5:

> In a 2012 *Telegraph* interview, Dennis Kelly argued that his 'characters know right from wrong' and are 'trying to make the best of a bad situation'. I would argue, however, that some characters' behaviour is deliberately brutal and immoral. There appears to be a clear disconnect between Kelly's view of his creations and the audience's view. For example, when Cathy threatens to 'gouge one of [Adam's] eyes out', we see not an action of someone trying to find a solution, rather the behaviour of a callous and sadistic individual. Kelly uses the grotesque dynamic verb 'gouge' because it implies a determined effort to inflict lasting damage. With the repetition of the plosive 'g' sounds, it's almost as if the audience can hear the eyeball being ripped out. Cathy's vicious actions clearly undermine Kelly's opinion that his characters 'know right from wrong'.

This is a really impressive paragraph. It includes:

- Relevant context, linked to the question.
- Close analysis of language, linked back to the context.
- Ambitious vocabulary.
- An evaluation of the writer's intentions.

So, now the student needs to (a) memorise sections of the paragraph and (b) practise tweaking it for similar exam questions.

For example, could the student fit this paragraph into a question where, instead of morality, the key theme is:

- Behaviour?
- Bullying?
- Human nature?
- Violence?
- Power?
- Strong and vulnerable characters?
- Conflict?
- Gangs/groups?
- Good and evil?

Yes! After a bit of thought and practice the student has easily recycled this paragraph for the question on human nature:

> In a 2012 *Telegraph* interview, Dennis Kelly argued that his 'characters know right from wrong' and are 'trying to make the best of a bad situation'. I would argue, however, that some characters' brutal and immoral behaviour is evidence of the dark side of human nature. There appears to be a clear disconnect between Kelly's view of his creations and the audience's view. For example, when Cathy threatens to 'gouge one of [Adam's] eyes out', we see not an action of someone trying to find a solution, rather the behaviour of a callous and sadistic individual. Kelly uses the grotesque dynamic verb 'gouge' because it implies a determined effort to inflict lasting damage. With the repetition of the plosive 'g' sounds, it's almost as if the audience can hear the eyeball being ripped out. Cathy's vicious actions clearly undermine Kelly's opinion about human nature, creating characters who appear not to 'know right from wrong'.

Now let's look at an example from *Macbeth*:

How does Shakespeare present ideas about loyalty in *Macbeth*?

> Through his construction of Lady Macbeth's conspiratorial character, Shakespeare emphasises how the appearance of loyalty can be used to conceal darker intents. The imperative 'look like th'innocent flower, But be the serpent under't' illustrates the unusual power balance between the couple, with the wife urging the husband to take action. The simile employs the soothing pastoral imagery of the 'flower' yet encourages Macbeth to adopt a 'serpent'-like course in reality. The Biblical allusion of the snake underlines Lady Macbeth's insistence that her husband must follow a path of Satanic disloyalty in order to achieve his kingly ambitions.

Next, the student has thought about how this paragraph might fit a question with a similar focus:

- Ambition
- Regicide
- Kingship
- Betrayal
- Deceit
- Doubt and indecision
- Equivocation
- Power
- Good and evil

As a result, the loyalty paragraph has been re-worked to fit the doubt and indecision question:

> Through his construction of Lady Macbeth's conspiratorial character, Shakespeare emphasises her role in persuading him to overcome his feelings of uncertainty and indecision about the morality of regicide. The imperative 'look like th'innocent flower, But be the serpent under't' illustrates the unusual power balance between the couple, with the wife urging the husband to stop procrastinating and take action. The simile employs the soothing pastoral imagery of the 'flower' yet encourages Macbeth to adopt a 'serpent'-like course in reality. The Biblical allusion of the snake underlines Lady Macbeth's insistence that her husband must follow a decisive path of Satanic disloyalty in order to achieve his kingly ambitions.

What if my prepared essay paragraphs don't fit the question?

Sometimes, you will read a question and panic. We didn't study this theme! My quotes and planned paragraphs won't fit! This is a nightmare!

I've been there.

I've sat in English exams and had a minute of anxiety and perspiration. Fortunately, I composed myself and remembered my teacher's wise words: *questions are there to be taken on. If you don't like the wording of a question, flip it on its head.*

For example, questions about power can also focus on characters that have no power. Or we can carefully consider wider meanings of the key word.

So, a question about 'responsibility' can focus on 1) who is responsible – to blame – for things that have happened?, 2) characters feeling guilty about their actions, 3) authority, control, leadership, 4) a specific job or duty and 5) sensible or mature behaviour.

This gives you much more to write about than just thinking about one narrow idea or theme.

Here's another example of how you might re-frame a typical GCSE English Literature question:

How does _____ present conflict in _____?

Depending on which text you're studying, conflict could refer to:

- Physical violence
- Psychological confusion
- Inner conflict
- Appearance versus reality
- Past versus present
- Binary opposites
- Prejudice/oppression
- Man versus nature
- Dreams versus reality

Looking at questions in this way gives you a much greater chance of being able to use your planned essay. But to be on the safe side, it's an excellent idea to build up a bank of prepared essays.

A student studying *An Inspector Calls*, for example, might have three ready-to-go essays that cover the following theme questions:

ESSAY 1
Class
Social obligations
Worker's rights
Socialism

ESSAY 2
The supernatural
Responsibility
Consequences of
actions

ESSAY 3
Morality
Generational conflict
Social change
Gender

As the Venn diagram suggests, the student has noticed that there are overlaps between some of these themes. This means they should be able to 'borrow' paragraphs from the essays, depending on the type of extract or exact wording of the question.

Conclusions

In English exams, time passes quickly. You don't get the time to write a detailed conclusion. For this reason, many students don't bother. They analyse right up until the clock, often finishing mid-sentence. The main body of your essay is the most important part. It will form the bulk of your marks. But a neat, concise conclusion can beautifully sum up your opinion of the question.

I get my students to make a couple of quick points at the end of their essay:

1. Refer back to the key word in the question, summing up your ideas about the importance of that theme or character in the text.

2. Explain, once more, the author's intention. What message were they trying to give about society?

Take a look at this example conclusion for a *Jekyll and Hyde* question:

How does Stevenson present Hyde as a terrifying monster?

1 — Stevenson's portrayal of Hyde as a 'detestable' and disturbing monster seems to emphasise his difference from society, but actually serves to remind us of the monster that 'hides' within all mankind. In doing so, Stevenson implies that the real monster isn't Hyde. Instead, it's the oppressive, reputation-

2 — obsessed Victorian society that prevented individuals from being free to express their true desires.

Can I plan these in advance as well?

Of course. As with the introductions and main paragraphs, conclusions can be crafted before the day and adapted to fit different questions. Get these nailed down and memorised and you'll soon be nearing the end of your essay writing revision!

❝ Top 5 to thrive

1. Make sure your essays include the key ingredients.

2. Prepare high-quality practice paragraphs and full essays in advance.

3. Plan introductions, main body paragraphs and conclusions, using my structures and examples if you're stuck.

4. Think carefully about which questions are similar to each other, which allows you to use a similar response.

5. Try to widen the meaning of the question so you can play to your strengths.

❞

Getting ready for the unseen texts

Students often worry about starting revision for English literature. But at least most of them have a rough understanding of some of the things they need to do: know the plot; understand the characters and themes; memorise quotes.

Yet, when it comes to unseen texts many students feel really concerned. They don't know where to begin. I've seen very confident students tremble at the prospect of preparing for a section of the exam on something they've *never studied before*!

There's no need for you to feel anxious about the unseen questions. There are things that you can do to help you feel more prepared for unseen texts. I'm going to share a few tricks that I think will leave you feeling ready to tackle anything that's thrown at you.

What unseen sections do I need to plan for?

GCSE English Literature

Most of the exam boards give students two unseen poems and ask them to analyse and compare them. If your school does OCR for English literature, you won't need to do this. Instead, you'll need to compare unseen prose (an extract from a novel) with an extract from the modern text that you have studied:

Exam board	Compare unseen poems?	Compare unseen prose with text you study?
AQA	✓	✗
Eduqas	✓	✗
OCR	✗	✓
Edexcel	✓	✗

GCSE English Language

All of the exam boards have one GCSE English language paper that gives students questions about two unseen non-fiction texts. The other GCSE English language paper focuses on unseen fiction. Three of the exam boards give you one unseen fiction text, but OCR asks you to compare two:

Exam board	Unseen fiction task
AQA	1 extract – no comparison
Eduqas	1 extract – no comparison
OCR	2 extracts – comparison required
Edexcel	1 extract – no comparison

How can I prepare for unseen poetry?

Tackling poems that you haven't studied before can seem intimidating. Many students find poetry difficult. They often see it as confusing and hard to work out. They struggle with the abstract ideas. They sometimes fail to spot the main themes.

As with all other revision, however, practice is vital. The more unseen poems you look at, the more confident you will feel about the exam, especially if you have a routine that helps you look for clues. Here's the step-by-step guide I suggest to my students:

A step-by-step guide to unseen poems

✔ Read the poem at least twice

✔ Titles are important

✔ So are final lines

✔ Devices/techniques matter

✔ But the effect is most important

✔ Link effect to deeper themes/symbolism

✔ Structure – where's the volta?

✔ If in doubt, use hedging language

To begin with, **read the poem carefully** without making any annotations. Try not to jump to any conclusions about the poem's meaning on this first reading. Read the question, as this should give you a clue about the poem's key themes. On the second reading, pick out interesting words, devices or structure. Don't attempt to do a line-by-line summary or 'translation' of the poem. Pick out four or five parts that grab your attention. Make sure these are linked to the question.

Poets think long and hard about **the title** they use for a poem. Look at it carefully. It should give you an indication about the main ideas behind the poem.

The same goes for **final lines**. These often act as a conclusion that summarises the main idea of the poem. Good final lines are usually thought-provoking and can surprise the reader.

Poems generally make use of figurative language and other interesting **poetic devices** such as rhyme and enjambment. Knowing these techniques can really help your understanding of the poet's intentions, BUT...

Being able to spot different language features and devices is useless without a **clear explanation of their effect**. The most important part of your analysis is explaining the impact of the writer's choices.

Once you've read the poem a few times and thought about the poet's methods, you can start to consider the possible meaning of the poem. Start off with some obvious questions. What happens in the poem? What are the speaker's feelings? What does it seem to be about? Then you can dig beneath the surface and **look for deeper meaning**: what is it really about?

Students often forget to write about the structure of the poem. Or they make vague comments about how the poem looks on the page, which doesn't pick up good marks. A more sophisticated way to write about structure is to **focus on the volta**. The volta (Italian for 'turn') is the part, found in many poems, where the tone or thoughts change. Looking at this section of a poem can help you understand shifts in mood or atmosphere.

If you're not sure about the true meaning of a poem, it's better to be cautious than trying to sound definite and possibly getting it badly wrong. If in doubt, use **hedging language** (words and phrases like 'perhaps', 'possibly', 'could be argued') to be on the safe side.

Putting it into practice

Let's have a look at a practice unseen poetry question:

In 'The Send-Off', how does the poet present the speaker's feelings about the men going off to war?

The Send-Off

Down the close, darkening lanes they sang their way
To the siding-shed,
And lined the train with faces grimly gay.

Their breasts were stuck all white with wreath and spray
As men's are, dead.

Dull porters watched them, and a casual tramp
Stood staring hard,
Sorry to miss them from the upland camp.
Then, unmoved, signals nodded, and a lamp
Winked to the guard.

So secretly, like wrongs hushed-up, they went.
They were not ours:
We never heard to which front these were sent.

Nor there if they yet mock what women meant
Who gave them flowers.

Shall they return to beatings of great bells
In wild trainloads?
A few, a few, too few for drums and yells,
May creep back, silent, to still village wells
Up half-known roads.

Wilfred Owen

- **Reading the poem twice** should help you notice things like the dark ('darkening lanes') and light ('white', 'lamp') imagery. There's also a motif of concealment, suggested by words and phrases such as 'winked', 'secretly', 'hushed-up', 'we never heard', 'creep back, silent' and 'half-known'. Is the government keeping quiet about the murky fate of the men they send to war?

- On the surface, **the title** 'The Send-Off' evokes an image of celebration. The departing soldiers are treated as heroes and lots of people turn up to wave them off. Yet, it's an ambiguous phrase. If someone is 'sent' somewhere it is usually an instruction or an order from a higher authority. It suggests a lack of choice. Also, funerals are often colloquially known as 'send-offs', reinforcing the idea that many of the soldiers are heading to their deaths.

- The soldier's fate is uncertain in **the final lines**. They 'may' return. If they do, they will do so without the fanfare of the 'send-off' to war. They will 'creep back, silent', implying that they will return feeling not heroism but instead shame. Or perhaps 'creep' highlights how their bodies will be broken. Either way, the horrors of the war will have changed them forever. They won't fully recognise the place to which they are returning.

- Some interesting **poetic devices**: the oxymoron 'grimly gay' indicates that the soldiers have a sense of their unhappy destiny. The personified 'wink[ing] lamp', which seems to be in on the unpleasant secret of what's to come. The repetition of 'few' in the final stanza.

- **The effect on the reader** of the repetition of 'few' is important. By emphasising the small number that will return, Owen highlights the significant human cost of war. 'A few' becomes 'too few', shifting the repetition to a specific criticism of the powers who send these young men off to their deaths.

- The poem uses the idea of young men heading off to war being treated with admiration and respect. Yet, as the poem concludes, we see **the deeper meaning**. These heralded soldiers will not return to a hero's welcome. If they return – and that's a big if – they will be broken and forgotten, a dirty secret to be hushed-up. In order to send more men to battle, the government must ignore the inconvenient truth of the casualties who return.

- There is a clear shift in tone with **the volta**: 'They were not ours'. Before the volta, the soldiers 'belong' to the crowds who are waving them goodbye. After this structural shift, we discover the reality of the situation. They will be lost to war. They will be forever changed by war. Perhaps they were never 'ours' in the first place.

- Look at my example of **hedging language** in the last sentence above. My use of 'perhaps' shows that I'm not absolutely certain about this interpretation. It's an interesting idea but I'm being cautious with my language.

Use this approach with all the practice unseen questions that you do in class and during revision.

What about introductions?

Remember the approach that I showed you to poetry introductions in the last chapter? Well, this method can also be used for unseen poetry:

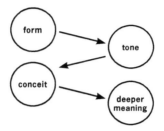

Applying this model to 'The Send-Off':

Deeper meaning

In 'The Send-Off', Owen uses the _didactic form_ to reveal the human cost that is hidden by the scenes of celebration as soldiers leave for war. The speaker adopts a _solemn and ironic tone_ to contrast the glorious yet hesitant departure with the almost shameful return of broken men. Through the _conceit of the journey_ with an uncertain destination, Owen _criticises the powerful men_ who send them off to the bleak battlefields, and _exposes the gloomy futures_ of the 'few' who return.

How can I prepare for unseen prose extracts?

Revising for unseen prose extracts

Practise:

✔ Answering questions on texts from different dates and genres.

✔ Exploding quotes that contain interesting language.

✔ Looking at structure carefully: beginning, end, structural shift.

✔ Identifying the precise effect of both language and structure.

✔ Thinking about the writer's intentions and whether they are successful.

Use practice papers that include extracts from 19th, 20th and 21st century texts. This will give you the experience of being able to write about texts that include different types of language and different narrative techniques from across the ages. Make sure you use extracts from a range of genres, so you don't struggle if you encounter a text of a type you haven't read before.

Pick out language features and powerful words that catch your eye. Explode these quotes, unpacking the techniques and choosing synonyms for key words.

Think about the **overall structure of the text**. What happens at the beginning of the text? What happens at the end? Are there any patterns (images/themes/ideas)? What has changed or stayed the same?

For both language and structure, you'll need to **be specific about the precise impact of the devices** on the reader. Do not use vague phrases like 'makes the reader want to read on' or 'grabs the reader's interest'.

The evaluation questions expect you to **consider whether the writer has created a successful piece of writing**. These usually ask you to focus on how the writer has built tension, described a character or setting, or created an atmosphere.

Putting it into practice

Let's have a look at a practice extract, from Chapter 2 of *Dracula* (1897) by Bram Stoker:

> By this time I had finished my supper, and by my host's desire had drawn up a chair by the fire and begun to smoke a cigar which he offered me, at the same time excusing himself that he did not smoke. I had now an opportunity of observing him, and found him of a very marked physiognomy.
>
> His face was a strong, a very strong, aquiline, with high bridge of the thin nose and peculiarly arched nostrils, with lofty domed forehead, and hair growing scantily round the temples but profusely elsewhere. His eyebrows were very massive, almost meeting over the nose, and with bushy hair that seemed to curl in its own profusion. The mouth, so far as I could see it under the heavy moustache, was fixed and rather cruel-looking, with peculiarly sharp white teeth. These protruded over the lips, whose remarkable ruddiness showed astonishing vitality in a man of his years. For the rest, his ears were pale, and at the tops extremely pointed. The chin was broad and strong, and the cheeks firm though thin. The general effect was one of extraordinary pallor.

Hitherto I had noticed the backs of his hands as they lay on his knees in the firelight, and they had seemed rather white and fine. But seeing them now close to me, I could not but notice that they were rather coarse, broad, with squat fingers. Strange to say, there were hairs in the centre of the palm. The nails were long and fine, and cut to a sharp point. As the Count leaned over me and his hands touched me, I could not repress a shudder. It may have been that his breath was rank, but a horrible feeling of nausea came over me, which, do what I would, I could not conceal.

The Count, evidently noticing it, drew back. And with a grim sort of smile, which showed more than he had yet done his protuberant teeth, sat himself down again on his own side of the fireplace. We were both silent for a while, and as I looked towards the window I saw the first dim streak of the coming dawn. There seemed a strange stillness over everything. But as I listened, I heard as if from down below in the valley the howling of many wolves. The Count's eyes gleamed, and he said.

"Listen to them, the children of the night. What music they make!" Seeing, I suppose, some expression in my face strange to him, he added, "Ah, sir, you dwellers in the city cannot enter into the feelings of the hunter."

Language: example exploded quote

The verb 'fixed' is associated with something that is unable or unwilling to move. As well as suggesting the strength of his bite, it could also imply that his evil character will not change.

'The mouth... was fixed and rather cruel-looking, with peculiarly sharp white teeth'

The noun 'white' usually suggests purity and innocence, but in this context they add to the Count's 'extraordinary pallor'. His unusual paleness indicates his supernatural, inhuman form.

His teeth are animalistic, which deepens the sense of fear, especially when linked to his fondness for the 'music' of the howling wolves.

Structure: example analysis

At the beginning of the extract Stoker focuses our attention on Dracula's beastly appearance: 'hair growing... profusely... His eyebrows were very massive... bushy hair that seemed to curl in its own profusion'. At this stage the reader shares Harker's sense of curiosity at the Count's unusual characteristics. By the end of the extract, Stoker has returned to the motif of animalism, using dialogue to express Dracula's unusual fondness for wolves, 'you dwellers in the city cannot enter into the feelings of the hunter'. This circular narrative helps the reader to recognise Harker's growing feelings of nervousness at the Count's predatory nature, which specifically links his unexplained hairiness with the wolves outside. The contrast between the inquisitive tone at the opening and the later tone of deep unease sparks feelings of concern on the reader's part. As a result of this significant structural shift, we are keen to discover what will happen now that Harker is apparently in close contact with a 'hunter' as intimidating as any creature.

Use this approach as part of your revision with each practice paper you attempt. The more papers you do at home, the more you will get the hang of picking out the important ideas and themes.

How can I prepare for unseen non-fiction extracts?

Revising for unseen non-fiction extracts

Practise:

✔ Answering questions about two texts on the same theme from different dates.

✔ Exploding quotes that contain interesting language.

✔ Identifying the precise effect of the language.

✔ Comparing similarities and differences in the writer's methods.

Putting it into practice

Let's have a look at a couple of short practice extracts:

TEXT A – *The Guardian* newspaper

'Mindblowing' haul of fossils over 500m years old unearthed in China

By Ian Sample, 21 March 2019

A "mindblowing" haul of fossils that captures the riot of evolution that kickstarted the diversity of life on Earth more than half a billion years ago has been discovered by researchers in China.

Palaeontologists found thousands of fossils in rocks on the bank of the Danshui river in Heubei province in southern China, where primitive forms of jellyfish, sponges, algae, anemones, worms and arthropods with thin whip-like feelers were entombed in an ancient underwater mudslide. The creatures are so well preserved in the fossils that the soft tissues of their bodies, including the muscles, guts, eyes, gills, mouths and other openings are all still visible. The 4,351 separate fossils excavated so far represent 101 species, 53 of them new.

"It is a huge surprise that such a large proportion of species in this fossil assemblage are new to science," said Robert Gaines, a geologist on the team from Pomona College in Claremont, California.

TEXT B – the *Bristol Mirror* newspaper

This extract introduces Mary Anning, a famous 19th century fossil finder

By George Cumberland, 11 January 1823

This persevering female has for years gone daily in search of fossil remains in importance at every tide, for many miles under the hanging cliffs at Lyme, whose fallen masses are her immediate object as they alone contain these valuable relics of a former world, which must be snatched at the moment of their fall, at the continual risk of being crushed by the half-suspended fragments they leave behind, or be left to be destroyed by the returning tide – to her exertions we owe nearly all the fine specimens of Ichthyosauri of the great collections.

The extraordinary thing in this young woman is that she has made herself so thoroughly acquainted with the science that the moment she finds any bones she knows to what tribe they belong. She fixes the bones on a frame with cement and then makes drawings and has them engraved… It is certainly a wonderful instance of divine favour – that this poor ignorant girl should be so blessed for by reading and application she arrived to that degree of knowledge as to be in the habit and writing and talking with professors and other clever men on the subject, and they all acknowledge that she understands more of the science than anyone else in the kingdom.

Comparing writer's methods: example plan

TEXT A

- Uses dynamic verbs to emphasise the importance of the fossils themselves:

'kickstarted the diversity of life on Earth'

- Adopts a tone of admiration for the work of the scientists:

'mindblowing haul'

- Uses a powerful metaphor to explain the scientific origin of fossils:

'riot of evolution'

TEXT B

- Uses **similar** dynamic verbs to highlight Anning's bravery and resourcefulness:

'must be snatched at the moment of their falling'

- **Also** displays admiration for Anning's work, but in **contrast** adopts a patronising tone:

'poor ignorant girl'

- Is **different** as the writer uses a Biblical allusion to imply Anning's talent was God-given:

'divine favour'

66 Top 5 to thrive

1. Check which parts of your GCSE English exams feature unseen texts.

2. Follow a step-by-step guide to each unseen poem you attempt.

3. For unseen poetry introductions, use my four-stage model.

4. Practise a variety of unseen prose extracts, focusing on language, structure and writer's intention.

5. Use a similar approach for non-fiction extracts, but also practise comparing writers' methods.

99

Preparing for the creative writing questions

For many of my students, creative writing is a struggle. When asked to come up with an interesting story, or a persuasive argument, or a clear explanation, their mind goes blank. They don't know how to structure it. They quickly run out of ideas. They end up making silly spelling mistakes. Even those who are confident creative writers can get stuck in an exam. Under pressure, they produce work that is unoriginal and flat.

Where most students go wrong with creative writing

Students often tell me that they're no good at creative writing. They see it as a talent. Something you can either do or not. What they don't realise is that creative writing is like anything else: the more you practise it, the better you get. And the easiest way to get better is to cut out the obvious mistakes that students make during the creative writing sections. Issues that crop up frequently during exams include:

Creative writing: 7 common mistakes to avoid

✗ Failing to do a brief plan before writing.

✗ Writing too much or too little.

✗ Lacking detail or development.

✗ No language features.

✗ Confusion of tenses.

✗ Not checking for spelling, punctuation and grammar (SPaG) errors.

✗ Paragraphs that don't link.

How can revision help overcome these issues?

A really helpful way of avoiding these mistakes is to take work that you've done during lessons, or in mock exams, and improve it at home.

Let's look at a narrative writing example:

18th Sept   _Write about a time when you had to make a quick exit_

It was a day like no other. The sun was shining brightly as I stepped onto the school bus. Birds were chirruping in the trees. Their were no clouds in the sky. It was peaceful and tranquil. A good time to be alive. I get off the bus and walk down the pavement to school, swerving around broken bottles and piles off dog poo. Not so nice after all, as I got closer to school.

There was a massive sign outside the front gates. Police warning: DO NOT ENTER! What was happening. Why all the fuss. I'm running back towards the bus when all of a sudden I here a voice on the loudspeaker. It told us to get out of the area. There was a massive gas leak and the whole thing could blow up, any minute now!

Back home, I took off my shoes and put my bag back on the floor. Sweat was dripping of me. My mum didn't believe me and was phoning the school when it came on the television. The cameras zoomed in on the sign. Phew. A day off school...

The student's first effort, done in class, falls into the seven traps of creative writing. The teacher has given the piece back and has highlighted a few of these errors:

18th Sept   _Write about a time when you had to make a quick exit_

1. Changes from past to present tense – avoid doing this in the same paragraph, as it confuses your reader.

It was a day like no other. The sun was shining brightly as I stepped onto the school bus. Birds were chirruping in the trees. Their were no clouds in the sky. It was peaceful and tranquil. A good time to be alive. I get off the bus and walk down the pavement to school, swerving around broken bottles and piles off dog poo. Not so nice after all, as I got closer to school.

2. SPaG mistakes – the homophones 'their/ there' and 'of/off'.

There was a massive sign outside the front gates. Police warning: DO NOT ENTER! What was happening. Why all the fuss. I'm running back towards the bus when all of a sudden I here a voice on the loudspeaker. <u>It told us to get out of the area</u>. There was a massive gas leak and the whole thing could blow up, <u>any minute now!</u>

3. Paragraphs don't link – the narrative jumps on quickly without explanation.

<u>Back home</u>, I took off my shoes and put my bag back on the floor. <u>Sweat was dripping off me</u>. My mum didn't believe me and was phoning the school when it came on the television. The cameras zoomed in on the sign. Phew. A day off school...

4. Opportunities to use language features are missed.

Then, the student spends time working on these issues during revision, and a couple of other SPaG mistakes they notice, making the following improvements:

It was a day like no other. The sun was shining brightly as I stepped onto the school bus. Birds were chirruping in the trees. There were no clouds in the sky. It was peaceful and tranquil. A good time to be alive. I got off the bus and walked down the pavement to school, swerving around broken bottles and piles of dog poo. Not so nice after all, as I got closer to school.

There was a massive sign outside the front gates. Police warning: DO NOT ENTER! What was happening? Why all the fuss? I ran back towards the bus when all of a sudden the angry loudspeaker pushed us back from the scene. There was a massive gas leak and the whole thing could blow up, any minute now!

I sprinted back home. I took off my shoes and put my bag back on the floor. The sweat on my forehead glistened like the morning dew. My mum didn't believe me and was phoning the school when it came on the television. The cameras zoomed in on the sign. Phew. A day off school...

The new draft isn't brilliant. But it's a definite improvement.

Over time, the student works at this draft, showing it to their teacher for further advice, then making gradual improvements. Eventually, it transforms into this:

Monday 4th May 2017. A day like no other. The sun's rays dazzled my bleary eyes. Birds chirruped complacently in the trees. A humid day, with patches of grey in an otherwise confident sky. All was peaceful and tranquil; a good time to be alive. Walking down the pavement to school, I swerved broken bottles and dodged dog faeces. The sun ducked behind the clouds, as I edged closer to school.

A massive sign acted as a cordon to the front gates: Police warning – DO NOT ENTER!

What was happening? What was all the fuss? From nowhere, an angry loudspeaker pushed us back from the scene. Panic. A silent and invisible foe. A gas leak. One wrong step and:

A spark creates a flame. A flame creates an explosion. An explosion crushes buildings like an angry giant.

I sprinted back home. Dropping my bag to the floor, my lungs gasped for breath. The sweat on my forehead glistened like crepuscular dew. My mum – dubious and disbelieving – phoned the school. But then she saw the television. She dropped the phone. A screen shattered across the floor. The cameras zoomed in on faces of fear. Scenes of total devastation...

This piece of writing still isn't complete. It's too short and lacks detail and development. Ideally, the finished piece should be between 2–3 sides of A4 (depending on the size of your handwriting).

But it's come a long way from the initial draft done in the classroom. That's the power of revision. It's not just about memorising things. As well as knowing more stuff, it's about getting better at things you'll need to do in the English exam.

But how exactly did the student improve the work?

Using the teacher's feedback, they worked on things like:

- **Improving boring sentences using language features and ambitious vocabulary**

  The sentence 'my mum didn't believe me' became 'my mum – dubious and disbelieving – '. This also includes alliteration and a more interesting sentence structure that can be used in any piece of writing. All you need to do is add detail by interrupting a sentence with a pair of dashes:
  - The dog walked towards me.

    The dog – a large, dark thing with menacing claws – walked towards me.
  - The hotel was on the edge of town.

    The hotel – an ugly 1960s building with dirty windows – was on the edge of town.

  Using a thesaurus allowed the student to find impressive words. They decided to transform the dull sentence 'the sweat was dripping off me' by using a simile. At one stage, they changed this line to 'the sweat on my forehead glistened like twilight dew'. Then the student looked up 'twilight' in a thesaurus and found the more striking 'crepuscular' instead.

- **Thinking carefully about the structure of the narrative**

  The original story starts with a happy, peaceful scene. This is suddenly interrupted with a dangerous event. The latest draft uses the same start but gives the reader clues that something bad is about to happen. The 'patches of grey' suggest darker times ahead. The 'complacent' birds aren't aware of the peril they face. The sun ducks 'behind the clouds' as if it's protecting itself from what's about to happen. This foreshadowing of later events makes the story much more structurally interesting.

This is really helpful but I'm still worried about the exam

Practising writing helps you get better at writing. But I do appreciate that not knowing the focus of the writing tasks can be intimidating. So, what if I told you that there is a way you can prepare for these unseen narrative/descriptive tasks? A way to ensure that you could go into the exam having a really good idea about what you're going to write *before* you enter.

Just like the pre-prepared literature essay from Chapter 7, I'm going to show you how to have a story up your sleeve (metaphorically please – I don't want you to get disqualified for cheating!) as you walk into the exam.

Planning narrative and descriptive writing in advance

✔ Write the correct amount.

✔ Make the question work for you.

✔ Use a frame story.

✔ Plan two or three well-written and well-structured pieces.

✔ Memorise your story (or the best parts at least).

Planning a story or description in advance during revision means that you can make it really good before you head into the exam room. You can make sure it's the right length. You can make sure you've spelt tricky words (and some easy ones!) correctly. You can make sure it's got an interesting structure.

In other words, you can avoid the traps that many students fall into. If you're a confident writer who prefers to come up with a detailed plan for a creative piece on the day, then that's great. But if you tend to struggle, you'll probably want to plan as much as possible before the exam itself.

What if my story doesn't fit the task?

My students are often concerned that they won't be able to make a pre-planned story fit with the question. *How can you plan ahead when you don't know what the task will be?* they ask.

Well, the good news is that the story and description prompts tend to be wide open. By this, I mean that they are usually general rather than specific.

The student's original task was to: **write about a time when you had to make a quick exit**. Let's look at some recent exam board tasks and tick which ones could be made to fit the original question:

Imaginative writing tasks from past papers

AQA

- Writing a description of an old person (using an image as a stimulus).
- Writing a story about when things turned out unexpectedly. ✓

Edexcel

- Writing about a time when you, or a person you know, did something that they shouldn't have done. ✓
- Writing about a secret (using an image as a potential stimulus).

Eduqas

- Continuing a story which starts 'It really wasn't the result I was looking for.' ✓
- Writing a story entitled 'Grandma'.
- Writing about when you had to go shopping with a relative. ✓
- Writing a story with the ending '… and I felt so sorry for myself.' ✓

OCR

- Using 'Hunger satisfied' as the title for a story.
- Writing about when you were waiting for something. ✓

An example: making the question work for you

Some of the tasks above could be used quite easily for the pre-planned story the student wrote during revision.

For example, 'things turned out unexpectedly' or 'someone did something they should not have done' could use the exact same response. Others might need a bit of adapting, such as this opening to the 'shopping with a relative' prompt:

> Saturday 9th May 2017. A day like no other. The sun's rays dazzled our bleary eyes, as we left the house. Birds chirruped complacently in the trees. A humid day, with patches of grey in an otherwise confident sky. All was peaceful and tranquil; a perfect time for a father and son shopping expedition. Walking down the pavement towards town, we swerved broken bottles and dodged dog faeces. The sun ducked behind the clouds, as we edged closer to the shopping centre.
>
> A massive sign acted as a cordon to the front of the building:
>
> Police warning – DO NOT ENTER!

What if I get a tricky one?

I've hopefully shown you how simple it is to tinker with the wide open questions you tend to get. Especially when there is a choice of questions for each exam board.

But what if you get one that seems really specific? What can you do then?

Firstly, you can **think about the question in more abstract terms**, rather than going for the obvious meaning. Take a look at the 'hunger satisfied' question above. The student could adapt their story to describe a trip to a supermarket that goes badly wrong. Or they could think of 'hunger' in more metaphorical terms. A hunger to stay alive, for example. That might make it much easier to use the pre-prepared story.

Secondly, you can **use a frame story**. A frame story is where a writer uses a story to introduce another story. Think of the frame that goes around a picture. Robert Louis Stevenson uses a framing device at the start of *Jekyll and Hyde* (Enfield tells Utterson the story of witnessing Mr Hyde's behaviour). So does Mary Shelley in *Frankenstein* (Walton writes letters to his sister, telling Victor's story).

As part of your revision, you could practise using a frame story to introduce your 'real' pre-prepared story. Look how this might work with the story titled 'Grandma' above:

> The grandchildren gathered around the fire. Swaddled in warm towels, fresh from the bath, we waited for Grandma to tell us the story of how we nearly didn't exist. Reclining back in her favourite armchair, she began...
>
> Monday 4th May 1937. A day like no other. The sun's rays dazzled my bleary eyes. Birds chirruped complacently in the trees. A humid day, with patches of grey in an otherwise confident sky. All was peaceful and tranquil; a good time to be alive. Walking down the pavement to school, I swerved broken bottles and dodged dog faeces. The sun ducked behind the clouds, as I edged closer to school.
>
> A massive sign acted as a cordon to the front gates:
>
> Police warning – DO NOT ENTER!

Thirdly, if you're still worried you might not be able to adapt your story on the day then you can **pre-prepare two or three excellent stories** and choose the one that best suits the task.

But how will I remember it all?

Like every other part of your revision, pre-planning stories is best done early. This will give you plenty of time to keep on crafting your narratives. And it will also give you plenty of time to memorise your story, or at least the best parts of it.

In the same way that you can use flashcards to remember key quotes and exploded quotes, you can also use them to remember brilliant sentences or paragraphs:

Paragraph 1 of my story

> Monday 4th May 2017. A day like no other. The sun's rays dazzled my bleary eyes. Birds chirruped complacently in the trees. A humid day, with patches of grey in an otherwise confident sky. All was peaceful and tranquil; a good time to be alive. Walking down the pavement to school, I swerved broken bottles and dodged dog faeces. The sun ducked behind the clouds, as I edged closer to school.

Begin by seeing if you can recall the first line, then build up from there. Over time, you'll start to remember good chunks of it, especially the most effective sections. This way, you can take the pressure off yourself if you dread the story writing part of the exam.

What about transactional writing?

The mistakes at the start of this chapter are also frequently found in students' transactional writing. Transactional writing is the non-fiction writing that you cover in your other GCSE English language exam, where you are asked to write something like an article, a letter, a speech or a piece of travel writing.

Depending on the exam board you are taking, you could be asked to do one longer or two shorter pieces of writing. Some boards let you pick the question, while others don't give any choice.

It's very difficult to predict what topics the tasks will focus on. It all depends on the extracts they use in the reading section of the paper. So you might get a task about sport, music, science, homework or TV celebrities! For this reason, you can't pre-prepare your answers in the same way that you can with narrative or descriptive writing.

Is there anything I can do to revise for transactional writing?
Yes! You might not be able to pre-plan an actual response, but you can certainly make sure you've planned the structure and bits of content of your piece.

Preparing language features and impressive phrases
Good writers have a dirty secret about how they get better at writing: they steal ideas from brilliant writers! If you read a really good phrase, a striking simile, or an imaginative metaphor, then I encourage you to do the same. These can be adapted to fit most topics. Imagine, for example, that you read this in a newspaper article:

> Allowing 16-year-olds to vote in a general election is like giving them a loaded gun. They may think that they are ready for the responsibility but they are not aware of the dangers of misusing the power in their hands.

You could memorise this format and adapt it for a different argument:

> Allowing the older generation to make decisions about climate change is like giving them a loaded gun. They may think that they have the wisdom of age. But they haven't considered the long-term dangers of misusing the power in their hands. We'll be the ones cleaning up their bloody mess.

Using a planned structure for your transactional writing
For a newspaper or magazine article, I suggest my students follow a structure like this:
1. Interesting headline
2. Well-crafted sub-heading
3. Creative opening that sets the scene
4. Introduce argument
5. Develop argument using anadiplosis (a type of repetition where the end of one sentence becomes the start of the next sentence)
6. Provide further detail with evidence or anecdote
7. Conclude argument with a call to arms

Practising the structure during revision

Imagine that you are given the following task: write an article for a magazine stating whether you believe that energy drinks should be banned in schools. Here's how you could practise using this structure during revision:

1. **Interesting headline**
   A MONSTER PROBLEM

2. **Well-crafted sub-heading**
   Is it time to consign energy drinks to the bin?

3. **Creative opening that sets the scene**
   A teenage girls cracks open a large silver cylinder. Fizz. Gulp. Belch. Bouncing her way towards the school gate, she pushes past a group of Year 7s. Her eyes are wide; her mind is racing. She's feeling rejuvenated. But is she ready to focus on some tricky algebra?

4. **Introduce argument**
   In generations to come, people will look back and wonder what on earth we were doing. Energy drinks not only disrupt our children's concentration, they also set them up for a life of migraines and obesity. Each dangerous mouthful nudges the consumer one step closer to the cliff edge.

5. **Develop argument using anadiplosis**
   Too much caffeine and sugar can cause anxiety. Anxiety can cause insomnia. Insomnia can cause a young person to reach out desperately for a morning can of Monster. It's a terrible cycle.

6. **Provide further detail with evidence or anecdote**
   In 2016, the National Board of Health and Science found that excessive consumption of energy drinks can cause hyperactivity, especially in teenagers. Other experts, like Professor Mike Smart from Newcastle University, have argued that a nationwide ban is the only way to combat the threat posed by the product.

7. **Conclude argument with a call to arms**
   Now is the time to act. Now is the time to banish energy drinks for good. Now is the time to take back control… of our children's health.

Making the structure fit other topics

Next, practise adapting this structure to fit a totally different topic:

Write a newspaper article about the problem of road traffic accidents involving teenage drivers.

1. **Interesting headline**
   STARK STATISTICS FOR TEENAGE DRIVERS

2. **Well-crafted sub-heading**
   Is it time to raise the driving age to 21?

3. **Creative opening that sets the scene**
   A teenage girl slams down hard on the accelerator pedal. Rev. Screech. Squeal. Hurtling her way towards the fast lane, she flies past an elderly driver. Her eyes are wide; her mind is racing. She's full of adrenaline. But has she spotted the lorry braking in the distance?

4. **Introduce argument**
   In generations to come, people will look back and wonder what on earth we were doing. Teenage drivers are a danger to themselves and other innocent road users. Every licence given to an immature 17-year-old drives us closer to the cliff edge...

5. **Develop argument using anadiplosis**
   A lapse in concentration leads to a reckless move. A reckless move leads to a high-speed collision. A high-speed collision leads to another funeral for a naïve young driver.

6. **Provide further detail with evidence or anecdote**
   In 2016, the UK's Road Safety Association found that drivers aged 16–19 are 33% more likely to be involved in a fatal crash than drivers aged 40–49. Other experts, like Professor Mike Smart from Newcastle University, have argued that raising the age limit is the only way to reduce the worrying statistics.

7. **Conclude argument with a call to arms**
   Now is the time to act. Now is the time to put the brake on dangerous young drivers. Now is the time to take back control... of the steering wheel.

Top 5 to thrive

1. During revision, practise avoiding the most common creative writing errors.

2. Improve the writing you do in class by re-drafting it several times.

3. Pre-prepare narrative pieces ahead of the exam.

4. Memorise the best parts of your stories, using retrieval practice.

5. Plan your transactional writing by using a set structure that can be adapted to fit different tasks.

Taking care of yourself and coping with exams

To perform well in English exams, you'll need to know lots about the books that you study. But you'll also need to prepare yourself for coping with sitting exams in general. The best way to do this is to follow these six steps:

1. Get organised
2. Study in the right environment
3. Manage your exam worries
4. Exercise regularly
5. Take breaks and get enough sleep
6. Stay motivated and show resilience

Spending hours glued to your desk is not enough. To do really well and reach your true potential, you'll need to look after yourself and think carefully about getting the most out of your revision time. So far, I've spent a lot of time showing you how to focus on your English skills.

Now I'm going to guide you through the full revision and exam experience. We'll start by thinking about planning your schedule. We'll see what the research says about how you should revise, and how you can look after yourself during this hectic period.

Finally, we'll consider how you can keep going when it seems like things are getting on top of you.

1. Get organised

Researchers have found[1] that students who are organised are more likely to achieve their goals. These students tend to:

- **Create a study plan**
  Starting to revise can seem overwhelming. Especially if you've left it till late on in the GCSE course. Ideally, you'll have been doing little and often. But if you find yourself feeling overwhelmed, you need to break

the GCSE courses down into chunks of learning. A typical week of your English revision timetable may look something like this:

Monday	Tuesday	Wednesday	Thursday	Friday	Saturday	Sunday
'Singh Song!'	Importance of Mrs Birling in *An Inspector Calls?*	Language P1, Q3 practice	'Climbing My Grandfather'	Compare 'Follower' and 'The Farmer's Bride'	Language P1, Q4 practice	Unseen Poetry practice question
How is Benvolio presented as a peacekeeper?	Compare 'Eden Rock' and 'Walking Away'	How does Dickens present poverty and want in *A Christmas Carol?*	Language P3, Q3 practice	Language P2, Q5 practice	'When We Two Parted'	*A Christmas Carol* key quotes
An Inspector Calls – key context	Language P2, Q4 practice	'Letters from Yorkshire'	How does Shakespeare present honour in *Romeo and Juliet?*		Relationships poems – key context	

- **Check to see how it's going**
  Then, after a week of revision, successful students will monitor their progress and think about what went well and what didn't:

Monday	Tuesday	Wednesday	Thursday	Friday	Saturday	Sunday
'Singh Song!'	Importance of Mrs Birling in *An Inspector Calls?* ✓	Language P1, Q3 practice	'Climbing My Grandfather' ✓	Compare 'Follower' and 'The Farmer's Bride' ✓	Language P1, Q4 practice	Unseen Poetry practice question
How is Benvolio presented as a peacekeeper?	Compare 'Eden Rock' and 'Walking Away'	How does Dickens present poverty and want in *A Christmas Carol?*	Language P3, Q3 practice	Language P2, Q5 practice ✓	'When We Two Parted'	*A Christmas Carol* key quotes ✓
An Inspector Calls – key context ✓	Language P2, Q4 practice	'Letters from Yorkshire' ✓	How does Shakespeare present honour in *Romeo and Juliet?*		Relationships poems – key context	

Then they'll give themselves reminders and set new targets:

Things to work on:

- *Really struggling with 'Singh Song!' – speak to Mr Roberts on Monday.*
- *Understand Benvolio's role but need better quotes.*
- *'Romeo and Juliet' 'honour' introduction is weak – needs more work.*
- *Was absent when we did 'When We Two Parted' – get Tyler's quotes.*

- **Stick to the schedule**

There will be times when you really don't feel like doing any English revision. The sun's shining outside. There's an amazing new film at the cinema. An electronic device is tempting you.

Resisting these temptations is the key to success. Ignoring short-term fun for long-term gains is part of the revision process. Nobody likes it, but everybody has to do it! Start your revision as soon as you get home from school, or as soon as you wake up on a weekend and it'll be done before you know it. Then you can have guilt-free relaxation time later on in the evening.

2. Study in the right environment

Where's the best place to study? Library or canteen? In your room or on the kitchen table?

Revising in a really quiet place, on your own or with just one friend, might seem boring. But it's going to give you the **best possible environment for learning**. If you don't have your own room, or live in a hectic house with lots of relatives, then somewhere like a library will be the best place to concentrate.

My students often tell me that they prefer a busier atmosphere. They're fine with noise, they say. But the research into studying environments suggests that they're putting themselves at a disadvantage:

Noise: Learning scientists have found[2] that noise and learning do not go well together. Background noise interferes with thinking, particularly with children. You might not realise, but studies show noise can also increase stress and frustration.

Music: Listening to your favourite artist while studying might make you feel better but one recent study[3] compared students who revised in a quiet room to those who listened to music. In an exam, those who studied without music outperformed those with music by over 60%.

Mobile phone: Your smartphone can be a huge distraction during study. Research has shown[4] that having your phone on you, even when you aren't using it, has a negative impact on your learning. For that reason, when revising, leave your phone in a different room. Have it with you only during study breaks.

3. Cope with exam worries

Feeling nervous about exams is perfectly natural. When things really matter to us, we tend to feel the butterflies in our stomach. But some of us worry a lot more than others. Occasionally, this can interfere with our efforts and stop us performing to our potential.

In my experience, students who have worked hard, in class and at home, tend to feel less stressed about the upcoming exams. Knowing stuff breeds confidence. So, sticking to your revision plan is important.

What else can help me feel less anxious about my exams?

- **Tackle the topics you're most worried about**
  It's tempting, particularly at the start of revision, to spend time on the stuff that you're good at. But it's best to get stuck into the scary things first! Revising a poem you know inside out might feel good but it won't help much in the long run. And you'll always have your nightmare poems lurking in the background.

- **Don't keep putting things off**
  Finding excuses why you can't revise now will leave you less time to cover everything in the future. It's a damaging cycle that will make you feel worse. Get started and you'll soon be in the habit.

- **Focus on things that are in your control**
  Some things are out of your control. The poem on the exam paper. The Shakespeare extract that's used. Whether the grade boundaries are high or low. But there are lots of things you can control. How many times you've read the novel. The number of revision sessions you attend. The number of practice essays you did on Lady Macbeth. Focus on these things instead of concerning yourself with things that are out of your hands.

- **Control your breathing**
  If you feel panicked before or during the exam, close your eyes and take deep breaths. Drink water and focus on positive thoughts.

- **Visualise a positive exam experience**
  Visualisation is a relaxation technique where you imagine calming images in your mind.

To help with exam worries, picture yourself in the exam room. Sat at a desk, you're feeling relaxed, determined and confident. Think of it as a calm environment, quiet and a natural place for you to be. Link the exam room to other calm places in your life. Repeat this visualisation regularly throughout the exam period.

4. Exercise regularly

As well as giving you a sense of well-being and helping you sleep better, **physical exercise** might also contribute to better grades. Recent research[5] suggests a link between regular physical activity and brain cell growth. Other studies[6] have also shown a relationship between aerobic exercise and exam performance.

How much exercise should I be aiming for over the revision period?

The government advises that teenagers should make sure they do an average of 60 minutes of physical activity each day. This can be spread out across the day, but the exercise should make you breathe faster and feel warmer.

What kind of exercise counts?
- Running/quick walking
- Sports, such as football, badminton or netball
- Cycling
- Climbing
- Swimming
- Skating
- Practical PE lessons
- Dancing
- Gym workout

When it comes to the exam period, you will be spending lots of time sitting down, revising and doing exams. So if you want to stay healthy and feel good about yourself, then make sure you keep active at other points throughout the day.

5. Take breaks and get enough sleep

Taking breaks during revision is vital. Research has shown[7] that our attention to a study task is limited. After a certain point, we stop taking information in and our performance drops off dramatically. In this study, students who took a couple of brief breaks during the hour of study did better in tests than those who didn't.

So, to stay relaxed and focused, make sure you build the following into your study routine:

- A walk outside
- Getting up and stretching your legs and body
- Go for a healthy snack or drink
- Chat to a friend on the phone
- Do something creative or fun: a spot of doodling or dancing to music

When it comes to **sleep**, the evidence is pretty clear. An important recent study[8] found a direct link between sleep and academic performance. Students who made sure they slept well do better in tests and exams. This shouldn't come as a surprise to you. When you're tired you struggle to concentrate, struggle to remember things, struggle to think clearly. A can of energy drink might seem to wake you up, but the jolt of caffeine will wear off and you'll probably feel even worse afterwards.

This particular study found that students whose sleep was of a better quality, a longer duration, and was more consistent achieved better grades. Importantly, just getting a decent night's sleep the night before the exam wasn't enough. To really feel the benefit – and the researchers found that it could make a 25% difference in results – students needed to have good sleep habits for at least a week, and preferably a month, before exams.

So what sleep patterns are likely to make a difference to your results?

- Get 8–10 hours' sleep per night.
- Keep to a similar routine throughout the week. For example, don't make a habit of staying up very late at weekends, which confuses your body clock.
- In the hour before you go to bed, avoid screen time, loud noises, bright lights, exercise or studying. Your brain needs a calm routine to get ready for sleep. A bath and a dark, quiet bedroom will help settle you for sleep.

6. Stay motivated and show resilience

What are the best ways I can stay motivated during my GCSE English revision?

The first thing is to take the chance to notice how much you've improved at English over the course of the GCSEs. Studies have shown[9] that **performing better at a subject motivates you to want to study it further**. Increasingly, being able to remember more about the texts during retrieval practice should prompt you to keep going. If in doubt, ask your teacher for feedback on your practice paragraphs and essays. Seeing that you're on the right path will encourage you to complete more examples.

Don't give in if you find something difficult. Focusing on your own goals is key. Set yourself small targets along the way and treat yourself for achieving them. Avoid falling into the trap of comparing yourself with others. Stressing about whether someone else will do better than you is a waste of energy. Concentrate instead on knowing more and performing better than you did in previous tests. If you did badly in a mock exam, use this as a learning opportunity, rather than seeing it as a failure. There will inevitably be setbacks throughout your English GCSEs. But if you believe in yourself and keep going, even when you really don't feel like it, you'll get the rewards in the end.

 **Top 5 to thrive**

1. Create a revision timetable and keep track of how it's going.
2. Limit background noise and other distractions.
3. Focus only on the things that you can control.
4. Take revision breaks, exercise often and get enough sleep.
5. Concentrate on your own gradual improvement and keep going when you find things difficult.

A final word – you can do it!

When you first picked up this book, you may well have been struggling to get your head around English revision and may have felt unsure where to start.

So, you've now read this book and have tried out my tips and strategies. Hopefully, you don't feel like that anymore.

If, at any point, you do find yourself worrying about any aspect of the GCSE English exams, go back to the relevant section. Re-read the chapter and follow my step-by-step advice again. With plenty of practice, you will get there.

We've been on a journey together. You've followed my advice and you've worked hard. You've got every reason to feel confident when you finally walk into your English exams. Hold your nerve, do your best and make yourself proud.

You can't really revise for GCSE English, can you? Well, as you've just proved: yes. Yes, you can!

Mark Roberts

Glossary of terms

This list doesn't include all of the words that can be used in English exams, but you should find it a helpful start.

Abstract noun	A type of noun that refers to a thing that does not exist as an actual object.
	e.g. happiness, democracy, cruelty
Alliteration	The repetition of the same consonant sounds in words that are near to each other.
	e.g. 'O, she doth **t**each the **t**orches **t**o **b**urn **b**right'
Allusion	An unexplained reference to someone or something outside of the text. Writers usually use the following allusions:
	1. Biblical – references to people or events from the Bible
	2. Literary – references to other novels, plays or poems
	3. Classical – references to things like ancient Greek or Roman myths
	4. Cultural – references to things like movies, TV programmes, pop music
Anadiplosis	A type of repetition where the end of one sentence becomes the start of the next sentence.
	e.g. 'It was a great **day to be alive. To be alive** and breathing in the cool mountain air.'
Anaphora	The repetition of a word or phrase at the beginning of lines, sentences or clauses.
	e.g. '**In every** cry of every Man,
	In every Infants cry of fear,
	In every voice...'
Anecdote	Using a short story about a real-life incident to make a point.
	e.g. 'On my first day at Oxford University I sat next to a nervous young man at dinner. I would never have predicted that he would have gone on to become the Prime Minister.'
Caesura	A pause that breaks the rhythm in a line of poetry, created by a comma, full stop, semi-colon or dash.
	e.g. 'She walks in beauty, like the night'
Chiasmus	Where two or more clauses are balanced against each other by reversing their structure for effect.
	e.g. 'Let us never negotiate out of fear, but let us never fear to negotiate.' From a speech by American president John F. Kennedy.
Circular narrative	A narrative structure (also called cyclical narrative) where at the end of a text the writer returns to the setting, action or ideas from the beginning.
Colloquial language	Communication that is casual, informal and conversational.
	e.g. 'You wanna grab something to eat?'
Conceit	An extended metaphor that runs throughout a poem.
	e.g. 'In 'Ozymandias', the conceit of the broken, forgotten statue is used to illustrate how a tyrant's power is inevitably temporary.'

Connotations	A meaning implied by a word that goes beyond its literal meaning.
	e.g. 'The connotations of the word "jewel" suggest that Romeo sees Juliet as beautiful, rare and precious.'
Dramatic irony	A situation in a play where the audience is aware of something of which a character (or characters) is not aware.
Dynamic verb	A verb that shows continual or gradual action.
	e.g. 'The girl **grabbed** the phone from her friend.'
Enjambment	When a sentence or phrase runs over from one poetic line to the next.
	e.g. 'But huge and mighty forms, that do not live
	like living men, moved slowly through the mind
	by day, and were a trouble to my dreams.'
Foreshadowing	A structural feature where a writer gives clues about what is to come later in the story.
Form	The type of poem, which can often be defined by its structure (e.g. sonnet, limerick) or its style (e.g. ode, dramatic monologue). Overall poetic form is often categorised in these four ways:
	1. Narrative – poems telling a story, usually involving characters and a plot.
	2. Lyric – poems expressing strong feelings and emotions.
	3. Didactic – poems teaching the reader through a moral message.
	4. Mixed – poems using a combination of the forms above.
Hedging language	Language that expresses caution, indirectness or uncertainty.
	e.g. '**It could be argued** that at the start of the play, Romeo is **perhaps** more interested in the idea of love than actually being in love.'
Hyperbole	Extreme exaggeration.
	e.g. 'every idiot who goes about with "Merry Christmas" on his lips, should be **boiled with his own pudding.**'
Imagery	Descriptive language that appeals to the sense and helps the reader to better imagine the world of the text.
	e.g. 'a dense drizzly fog lay low upon the great city. Mud-coloured clouds drooped sadly over the muddy streets.'
Inciting incident	An event or plot point that thrusts the main character(s) to follow their mission.
	e.g. 'The inciting incident in An Inspector Calls is the arrival of the mysterious inspector.'
Metaphor	A word or phrase used to describe something as if it was something else.
	e.g. 'Juliet is the sun'
Motif	A recurring image, idea or symbol that develops or explains a theme.
	e.g. 'In Macbeth, the motif of blood is used to highlight feelings of constant guilt.'
Mouthpiece	A character who speaks on behalf of the author, and is used to reveal their views on a subject.
	e.g. 'It could be argued that in Of Mice and Men, at times George acts as a mouthpiece for Steinbeck's views on American society in the 1930s.'

Oxymoron	A phrase where two opposite ideas are joined to create an effect. e.g. 'exploding comfortably'
Paradox	An idea or statement that appears to be self-contradictory or make no sense, but that still reveals a hidden truth. e.g. 'Hamlet uses the paradox "I must be cruel, only to be kind" to justify his violent behaviour.'
Pastoral	Texts that are associated with pleasant aspects of rural life and nature. e.g. 'The speaker in "The Prelude" can no longer appreciate nature's pastoral elements: "no pleasant images of trees/Of sea or sky, no colours of green fields".'
Personification	A type of metaphor that makes something non-human seem human. e.g. '**dark night strangles** the travelling lamp'
Plosive	An abrupt sound made by closing the mouth then releasing air. Plosive sounds in English are B, P, T, K, G and D. When repeated they often give an impression of harshness and strong emotion. e.g. 'ice**d** eas**t** win**d**s tha**t** knive us'
Sentence function	The reason why a sentence has been used by a speaker. There are four types of sentence function: 1. Imperative – a command or instruction 2. Interrogative (?) – a question 3. Exclamatory (!) – expresses strong feelings 4. Declarative – makes a statement
Simile	Comparing two things by using 'like' or 'as'. e.g. 'It wasn't like a man, it was **like some damned Juggernaut**'
Stanza	A group of lines in poetry that form sections of the poem. Often called 'verse'.
Superlative	An adjective that expresses the highest or lowest quality of something. e.g. tallest, worst, most embarrassing
Theme	The central idea or ideas of a text. e.g. 'Jealousy and betrayal are key themes in *Othello*.'
Tone	The way a writer creates an attitude, mood or atmosphere in their writing. e.g. 'In "Porphyria's Lover", Browning uses a matter-of-fact, contented tone to reveal the disturbing attitudes of the speaker.'
Trope	Commonly recurring motifs or ideas that can be found in a particular genre or throughout a writer's works. e.g. 'In *Frankenstein*, Shelley uses the Gothic trope of The Sublime to emphasise the exciting yet dangerous power of nature.'
Volta	Italian for 'turn', this is the part of the poem where the tone or thoughts change. e.g. 'My name is Ozymandias, King of Kings; Look on my Works, ye Mighty, and despair! **Nothing beside remains**. Round the decay Of that colossal Wreck, boundless and bare The lone and level sands stretch far away.'

Endnotes

Chapter 1

Page 4 **1** Dunlosky, J., Rawson, K.A., Marsh, E.J., Nathan, M.J., & Willingham, D.T. (2013) 'Improving students' learning with effective learning techniques: promising directions from cognitive and educational psychology', *Psychological Science in the Public Interest*, 14:1, 4–58.

Chapter 3

Page 23 **1** For example, Haber, R.N. & Myers, B.L. (1982) 'Memory for pictograms, pictures, and words separately and all mixed up', *Perception*, 11:1, pp.57–64.

Page 25 **2** Curtis, C. (2019) *How to Teach English*, Crown House, Carmarthen, p.170.

Chapter 10

Page 92 **1** Martin, A.J. (2002) 'Motivation and academic resilience: developing a model of student enhancement', *Australian Journal of Education*, 46, 34–49.

Page 94 **2** Erickson, L.C. & Newman, R.S. (2017) 'Influences of background noise on infants and children', *Current Directions in Psychological Science*, 26:5, 451–457.

Page 95 **3** Currie, H. & Perham, N. (2014) 'Does listening to preferred music improve reading comprehension performance?', *Applied Cognitive Psychology*, 28, 279–284.

Page 95 **4** Mendoza, J.S., Pody, B.C., Lee, S., Kim, M., & McDonough, I.M. (2018) 'The effect of cellphones on attention and learning: The influences of time, distraction, and nomophobia', *Computers in Human Behaviour*, 86, 52–60.

Page 96 **5** Jack, C.R., Joyner, M.J. & Petersen, R.C. (2020) 'Cardiorespiratory fitness and brain volumes', *Mayo Clinic Proceedings*, 95:1, 6–8.

Page 96 **6** For example, Lees, C. & Hopkins, J. (2013) 'Effect of aerobic exercise on cognition, academic achievement, and psychosocial function in children: a systematic review of randomized control trials', *Preventing Chronic Disease*, 10, 174 and Singh, A., Uijtdewilligen, L., Twisk, J.W.R., van Mechelen, W., & Chinapaw, M.J.M. (2012) 'Physical activity and performance at school: a systematic review of the literature including a methodological quality assessment', *JAMA Pediatrics*, 166: 49–55.

Page 97 **7** Ariga, A. & Lleras, A. (2011) 'Brief and rare mental "breaks" keep you focused: Deactivation and reactivation of task goals preempt vigilance decrements', *Cognition*, 118:3, 439–443.

Page 97 **8** Okano, K., Kaczmarzyk, J.R., Dave, N., Gabrieli, J.D.E. & Grossman, J.C. (2019) 'Sleep quality, duration, and consistency are associated with better academic performance in college students', *NPJ Science of Learning*, 4:16, 1–5.

Page 98 **9** Garon-Carrier, G., Boivin, M., Guay, F. et al. (2015) 'Intrinsic motivation and achievement in mathematics in elementary school: A longitudinal investigation of their association', *Child Development* 87:1, 165–175.

Acknowledgements

The author and publisher are grateful to the copyright holders for permission to use quoted materials and images.

Cover image and page 1: © Shutterstock.com/rosewind; page 5, © Nick Moore / Alamy Stock Photo

Extract on page 77 from 'Mindblowing haul of fossils over 500m years old unearthed in China' by Ian Sample © The Guardian, 2019.

Quotations from An Inspector Calls taken from An Inspector Calls and Other Plays © J B Priestley 1948, 1950, published by Penguin Books 1969. Reproduced by permission of Penguin Books Ltd. © 2000.

Quotations from Animal Farm taken from Animal Farm © George Orwell, 1945, published by Penguin Books Ltd.

Quotations from Blood Brothers taken from Blood Brothers © Willy Russell, 2001, Methuen Drama, an imprint of Bloomsbury Publishing Plc. Reproduced by permission of Bloomsbury Publishing Plc.

Quotations from 'Bayonet Charge' taken from The Hawk in the Rain © Ted Hughes, 1957, published by Faber and Faber Ltd.

Quotations from DNA taken from DNA © Denis Kelly, 2008, published by Oberon Books Ltd. Reproduced by kind permission of Oberon Books.

Quotations from Lord of the Flies taken from Lord of the Flies © William Golding, 2005, Faber and Faber Ltd.

Every effort has been made to trace copyright holders and obtain their permission for the use of copyright material. The authors and publisher will gladly receive information enabling them to rectify any error or omission in subsequent editions.

All facts are correct at time of going to press.

Published by Collins
An imprint of HarperCollinsPublishers
1 London Bridge Street
London SE1 9GF

ISBN: 978-0-00-839280-2

First published 2020

10 9 8 7 6 5 4 3 2

©HarperCollinsPublishers Ltd. 2020

British Library Cataloguing in Publication Data.

A CIP record of this book is available from the British Library.

Publishers: Clare Souza and Katie Sergeant
Author: Mark Roberts
Project Management: Lauren Murray and Richard Toms
Cover Design: Sarah Duxbury
Inside Concept Design and Page Layout: Ian Wrigley
Production: Karen Nulty
Printed by: CPI Group (UK) Ltd, Croydon, CR0 4YY

MIX
Paper from responsible source

FSC
www.fsc.org

FSC® C007454

This book is produced from independently certified FSC™ paper to ensure responsible forest management.

For more information visit: www.harpercollins.co.uk/green